OPPORTUNITIES

in

12/05
12.95

E

OPPORTUNITIES

in

Engineering Careers

REVISED EDITION

NICHOLAS BASTA

VGM Career Books

*Chicago   New York   San Francisco   Lisbon   London   Madrid   Mexico City
Milan   New Delhi   San Juan   Seoul   Singapore   Sydney   Toronto*

Library of Congress Cataloging-in-Publication Data

Basta, Nicholas, 1954–
      Opportunities in engineering careers / Nicholas Basta.—Rev. ed.
         p.   cm.—(VGM opportunities series)
      Includes bibliographical references.
      ISBN 0-07-139046-4 (paperback)
      1. Engineering—Vocational guidance.   I. Title. II. Series.

TA157 .B342   2002
620′.0023—dc21   2002069186

1 2 3 4 5 6 7 8 9 0   LBM/LBM   1 0 9 8 7 6 5 4 3 2

ISBN 0-07-139046-4

McGraw-Hill books are available at special quantity discounts to use as premiums and sales promotions, or for use in corporate training programs. For more information, please write to the Director of Special Sales, Professional Publishing, McGraw-Hill, Two Penn Plaza, New York, NY 10121-2298. Or contact your local bookstore.

This book is printed on acid-free paper.

Contents

Foreword   vii

Acknowledgments   ix

Introduction   xi

1. Engineering: Gateway to the Technological World   1

The everyday impact of engineering. Profile of the
profession today. What is engineering? What engineers
do. Engineers and scientists. Engineering and
technology. Engineers and the world. Career options.
Women, minorities, and engineering.

2. The Common Elements of Engineering   27

Career opportunities and goals. Areas of work.
Education. Employment in the private and public
sectors. Engineers and computers. Salaries and the
intangible rewards.

3. Classic Engineering   43

Electrical/electronics engineering. Mechanical
engineering. Civil engineering. Chemical engineering.
Mining, metallurgical, and petroleum engineering.

4. Modern Engineering   101

Industrial/manufacturing engineering. Aerospace/
aeronautical engineering. Materials engineering.
Environmental engineering. Computer engineering.

5. Engineering Specialties   125

Biomedical/bioengineering. Agricultural engineering.
Nuclear engineering. Marine/ocean engineering and
naval architecture. Safety and fire protection engineering. Optical engineering. Other engineering specialties.

6. Engineering Technology   143

The pros and cons of engineering technology. Types of
engineering technology degrees. Work environments.

7. Engineering Education   151

The engineering curriculum. Choosing a school.
Alternatives to the four-year program. Financial aid.
What to do now.

Appendix A: Recommended Reading   163
Appendix B: Engineering and Technology
    Associations   165

Foreword

ENGINEERING IS BY far the largest of the scientific and technical professions. Indeed, of all professions, only elementary and secondary school teachers outnumber engineers. Given the sheer size of the field and the enormous variety of attractive positions open to its practitioners, one might expect that it would not be too difficult to find good information about engineering careers; in fact, however, it is not easy to find accurate guidance to the field. The abbreviated material in encyclopedias and such references as the *Occupational Outlook Handbook* are not bad, but people pondering lifetime commitments to a career deserve much more.

Thus it is a pleasure to introduce *Opportunities in Engineering Careers* to its readers. This guide is thorough: it covers the full range of career-related concerns, from information on engineering positions and the people in them to practical tips about engineering colleges, licensing and professional registration, and other steps along the way. It is even-handed: it discusses drawbacks as well as advantages of the field and avoids hype about the most trendy specialties, a common failing of other materials about the engineering profession. Most of all, it is wide-ranging: it touches on a full selection of all the different roles and achievements of engineers at work.

The diversity of the profession is astonishing. Nicholas Basta rightly begins with traditional engineering: the electrical engineers who create computers, communication networks, and power systems; the mechanical engineers who produce every sort of machinery; and the civil engineers who design bridges, highways, and other kinds of structures and systems. But he also pays attention to the countless other applications of modern engineering training. More than ever, engineers are moving into every area of the economy, including health care, finance and banking, and wholesale and retail trade. Moreover, engineering training is increasingly being seen as the "new form of liberal arts," applicable to many kinds of jobs and particularly crucial for management.

The very nature of engineering—that it deals with leading-edge technology—means that the profession is constantly changing. Engineers in the twenty-first century will deal with new materials, constantly accelerating applications of automation, miniaturization of an unprecedented nature, and all sorts of other marvels. They also will deal with a multinational world in which work groups can draw on personnel located across the globe. For those able to deal with the science and math on which all technology depends, few career choices will be able to surpass engineering. Here is a handbook for that future.

R. A. Ellis
Former Director of Research and Editor, *Engineers*
American Association of Engineering Societies

Acknowledgments

A CONSIDERABLE NUMBER of organizations and individuals provided assistance and advice in the creation of this book. They include the American Academy of Environmental Engineers; the Institute of Electrical and Electronics Engineers, Inc.; the American Society of Agricultural Engineers; the American Society of Mechanical Engineers; the American Society of Civil Engineers; the American Institute of Chemical Engineers; the American Society of Engineering Educators; the Institute of Industrial Engineers; the Society of Automotive Engineers; the Instrument Society of America; the American Society of Safety Engineers; the Society of Manufacturing Engineers; and the Junior Engineering Technical Society.

Matt Doster of the Engineering Workforce Commission, a group within the American Association of Engineering Societies, was generous in sharing the invaluable data that EWC collects. Finally, I would like to remember the late Betty M. Vetter, founder and director of the Commission on Professionals in Science and Technology (Washington, D.C.). For decades her group gathered data and produced studies that helped form the vibrant engineering professions that exist today.

Introduction

Do you like science? Would you like to translate that familiarity with science into faster computers, energy-efficient automobiles, wireless communication systems, economical homes, better health care, cleaner water and air, and food for a growing world population? The path is before you—study engineering in college.

Engineering is the key that opens the doors of nearly all types of technology. In fact, most of the elements of our increasingly technological society are the product of engineers' work. The traditional image of the field is of an engineer examining a gigantic iron machine in a dirty, noisy factory. Today's engineers, however, move in all sectors of society, from corporate headquarters to laboratories, spaceship runways, hospitals, even the halls of government. As technology has broadened its impact on how we live, it has created a wealth of careers for those who understand it.

Technology provides the tools by which humanity copes with the world around it. Yet, it is a bad word to many people who believe that technology is devastating our environment. It is true that the world is different today than it was fifty or a hundred years ago. The main difference, however, is that there are more than six billion people on the planet, and the seven-billion milestone will happen quite soon. Technology, today, means the difference between living and starving for billions of people. An intensifying debate is occurring over the value and impact of technology in our world, and there are engineers involved on every side of this debate.

Many engineers are involved every day with such staples of living as clean water, wholesome food, or power for heating and lighting. Many others, though, use their familiarity with technology in other ways. In industrialized nations such as the United States or Canada, people trained in engineering work in business management, financial services, government, the military, health care, entertainment, communications, and others. There are few professions or career choices that are excluded because of an engineering background; there are a surprising number for which an engineering background is a very desirable initiation. This book will illustrate many of them.

Engineering Disciplines

This book will introduce the engineering profession to you and describe the many types of engineers at work today. Engineering is not a profession or an academic program that was "set" years ago. It is evolving every year. Chapter 2, The Common Elements of Engineering, describes some basic engineering functions and job possibilities open to all types of engineers. The classic engineering disciplines, most of which were established in the nineteenth century, are described in Chapter 3. These disciplines are:

- electrical/electronic
- mechanical
- civil
- chemical
- mining, metallurgical, and petroleum

In the early years of the twentieth century—as the airplane, the automobile, and factory assembly lines changed the face of American industry—a new group of engineering disciplines arose. Later, after World War II, the advent of electronics, the computer, and nuclear power led to a diverse group of newer disciplines. These engineers are grouped in Chapter 4, Modern Engineering. They include:

- industrial/manufacturing
- aerospace
- materials/metallurgical, ceramic
- environmental
- computer

All these disciplines constitute the bulk of engineers being educated today. The smallest of these ten disciplines, the materials/metallurgical field, welcomed 901 B.S. graduates in 2000, according to the Engineering Workforce Commission (Washington, D.C.). The largest, mechanical, added 12,989 graduates.

But there are many additional types of engineers. Chapter 5, Engineering Specialties, provides a summary of the more notable disciplines:

- biomedical
- agricultural
- nuclear

- marine/ocean and naval architecture
- safety and fire protection
- optical
- automotive
- textile
- energy
- heating, ventilating, and air-conditioning
- systems/operations research
- engineering history/technical writing

Chapter 6, Engineering Technology, covers the variety of programs and work responsibilities for engineering/industrial technology graduates, a field closely associated with engineering.

The last section, Chapter 7, Engineering Education, provides details on the best ways to prepare for engineering study, how to select a school, and how to get your career off to the right start.

Profiles

Interspersed throughout the book are a number of profiles of working engineers. These profiles are part fiction, part fact. They are created as composites of real engineers, based on the author's twenty-five years of reporting on the engineering professions. Names, of course, have been changed. The engineering field is diverse and opportunities ever-changing, so it is not advisable to model your own career too closely after one of the profiles.

The actual work that engineers do is a vast mystery to most of us. It is rare for an engineer to be the subject of a television series or the hero of a novel. That's a shame because there is plenty of drama in designing and building a bridge or in testing a new aircraft. If nothing else, these profiles will give the flavor of engineering work.

1

Engineering: Gateway to the Technological World

TAKE A LOOK around yourself, no matter where you are sitting or standing as you read this. What do you see? You may see books, including this one that you are holding. Perhaps you see tables, chairs, and shelves if you are in a library. Maybe there is a couch, television set, telephone, windows, and walls if you are reading this book at home.

No matter what you see, you can be assured that an engineer was involved in designing or making it. Mechanical engineers helped make the machines that produced the paper this book is printed on; chemical engineers produced the ink of these words. Electronics and communications engineers develop the equipment and run the systems that provide television and telecommunications. Textile engineers manufactured the woven fabrics that make up your clothes; civil and materials engineers developed the paints, structural materials, and windows that make up the room around you. If you're in any kind of vehicle, many different engineers had a hand in designing and producing it.

The Everyday Impact of Engineering

These examples only scratch the surface of the activities and responsibilities of engineers. Engineering represents a group of skills that are central to modern life. Computers, aircraft, telecommunications, and all the other forms of high technology are obvious fruits of engineering practice. Not so obvious are the water we drink, the air we breathe, the houses we live in, even the food we eat. Individuals with training in engineering can gain entry into practically every form of business and the arts that make up our society.

Engineering offers the chance of lively, interesting work. More practically, it is one of the most reliable forms of employment. In recent years about half of the job offerings that campus recruitment offices report have gone to engineering students, even though they represent no more than 10 percent of graduates. Starting salaries for engineers are invariably the highest of any given to graduates with bachelor's degrees. Also, it is rare for the unemployment rate of engineers as a group to rise above a couple of percentage points, even when the economy is suffering.

In recent years the quality and quantity of engineers have been matters of national concern. Although most workers (of all types, from presidents to plumbers) are not in manufacturing, that sector of the economy is the driving force that sets all the other sectors in motion. The majority of engineers work either directly in manufacturing or construction, or in a host of services that support those activities. In today's world, nations generally are no longer competing militarily (thankfully!); instead, their economies compete through trade. The U.S. manufacturing base is the foundation of our success in competing in this arena. When the economy suffers, one of the first checkpoints for national policy makers is the health of the engineering professions. And as for those instances where the military is called to action, since the end of World War II, the United States has had a pre-eminent military infrastructure that has been supported by the efforts of thousands and thousands of civilian engineers. The technology developed for military applications has, in turn, translated into countless numbers of peaceful applications.

Besides its job security and its central position in the national economy, engineering often has opportunities for highly creative work. Most inventors have some type of engineering training. Think of the tremendous changes being wrought in our lifestyles by the introduction of the personal computer. Engineers were involved in the early days of computing and are at the forefront of developing everything from compact disks to the Internet for using computers today. Some engineers work in jobs that are highly routine, checking the same product characteristics day after day. But others are more involved in finding new ways to build or make things and in solving pressing social issues.

Something that sounds as good as engineering must have a catch, right? Well, there is no denying that engineering study is hard work. Engineering students must contend with a lot of math and science. Regardless of the type of engineering that interests you, it is based on various scientific discoveries, and to be a good engineer, you must be familiar with science.

Most engineering students, and many working engineers, must fight their image as nerds. The totally "out of it" apparel of the Dilbert cartoon character is emblematic. Some of the top college students, many of whom would make excellent engineers, choose to go on to law or business management simply because lawyers and executives have the reputation of higher status than engineers.

Another drawback is that although most American industries would cease to exist without engineers, those industries tend not to promote engineers as presidents or top executives. Backgrounds in finance or marketing are often preferred over engineering. This tendency is unusual. In both Germany and Japan, the two countries besides the United States that are renowned for their technological prowess, most major manufacturing companies are headed by engineers.

Profile of the Profession Today

Most of these disadvantages, however, are ones of perception, not of reality. Many leading U.S. companies have engineering managers. Although engineering is not an automatic ticket to upper management, it is certainly no impediment. And the nerdy image of engineering is one that is rapidly fading away. With more and more engineering work involving teams of experts solving manufacturing problems, the time is passing when an engineer could be a lone operator in a laboratory, spending more time with a computer than with fellow workers.

Fortunately, the status of engineers in the United States is changing. Managers with engineering backgrounds now hold many of the seats in corporate boardrooms. For example, Louis Gerstner, recently retired chairman of IBM, was educated as an engineer (and before taking the reins at IBM, he had been CEO of a consumer-goods company, RJR Nabisco). Craig Barrett, CEO of

Intel Corporation, is a Ph.D. materials engineer. And Garret Westerhof, CEO of the construction firm Malcolm Pirnie, has a civil engineering background. The global competitiveness that American manufacturers are developing is bringing the production and management roles—usually run by the engineering staff—into the forefront. Better engineering means better manufacturing, higher quality, and more innovation—all the things that American industry needs to succeed.

Engineering used to be thought of as a white, male club, but that time has gone, never to return. All the engineering branches are reaching out to women and minority groups. If you are in either category, engineering is opening its doors to you. There are professional organizations that offer support, and there are already many women and minority engineers who are rewriting the book on the American success story.

Finally, engineering is excellent preparation for tackling many of society's ills. The situation of the homeless cries out for a solution to the problem of affordable housing. The environment has become a global issue of the highest importance; engineering skills will be needed to make amends for the pollution of the past and to prevent new forms of pollution. Poverty is cured by jobs, and jobs are created when engineers develop new industries and tools. The problem of hunger can be confronted with more economical means of producing and delivering food.

This is a book to guide you in choices of engineering disciplines if you are already leaning toward engineering. And if you are not so inclined, it will show you why engineering might be your best choice. If mathematics and science are a snap for you to learn, engineering can be the best possible way to exercise that talent. Even if math and science are intimidating to you, don't automatically reject engineering. These hurdles can be overcome, and you will have a chance to apply a strong technical training in all sorts of interesting ways.

What Is Engineering?

Here is the formal definition of engineering, as espoused by the American Society for Engineering Education:

> Engineering is the profession in which a knowledge of the mathematical and natural sciences gained by study, experience and practice is applied with judgment to develop ways to utilize the materials and forces of nature economically for benefit of mankind.

This is a definition that was surely argued over and amended many times by a large number of people. Therefore every word in it has a precise meaning. The key words, as this engineer sees it, are these:

"Mathematical and Natural Sciences"

No getting around it: engineering involves a lot of math and science. In practice, however, most engineers don't work with any mathematics above calculus, which many students learn in their last year of high school or first year of college. More math is taught—such as linear algebra, differential equations, and so forth—because educators want to be sure that engineers are well grounded in mathematics at the outset of their careers. Mathematics beyond calculus is essential for engineers who go on to get a master's degree or doctorate. But don't be intimidated. Many engineers are very successful in their daily work with no mathematics beyond algebra.

The sciences are another story. One way or another, all engineers are involved with sciences such as chemistry, physics, geology, or materials—but not all sciences, and not all the time. This is a key difference between the profession of engineer and that of scientist.

"Study, Experience, and Practice"

Engineering combines art with science. "Art" means that the engineer depends on many things that haven't been reduced to mathematical equations. Engineers often depend on rules of thumb or calculated guesses. They work with approximations, with unknowns, and with their intuition and judgment. Nevertheless, the work must be on target—very often, lives are at stake in a bridge or aircraft design. That's why these structures are built with a margin of safety and are thoroughly tested before use.

"Economics"

This may be the most important, or at least the most distinctive, aspect of engineering. A doctor will spend whatever it takes to heal a sick person; a lawyer can continue fighting a cause in court until funds are exhausted. But an engineer, every day of his or her work life, is constantly battling to produce goods more efficiently, to save energy, to conserve resources and the environment, and to reduce wear and damage. The difference between a failed product and a wild success can be as little as fifty cents in production costs. Engineers are continually confronting economics.

The importance of economics led to this informal definition of engineering: *engineering is doing for one dollar what any darn fool can do for two*. Although money and economics may seem a boring focus in one's work, they are truly the exciting aspects of engineering. The next time you buy a can of soup, realize that it costs less today than it did 150 years ago when canned food was invented. And if you use a personal computer, realize that it has the same computing power, in a box costing a couple of thousand dollars, that a room-sized monster machine costing millions of dollars had in the 1960s. Smart engineering made the difference.

What Engineers Do

What do engineers do? They build bridges, design aircraft, run power plants and factories, and get ore from the ground. All these things are well known, but they are not the only tasks performed by engineers. Engineering work is as varied as the individuals who practice it.

Engineers not only design aircraft, for example, they also build them, test them, and fly them. That includes everything from satellites to blimps, gliders, or rockets. The first man on the moon, Neil Armstrong, was an engineer.

Engineers build bridges; they also build tunnels, highways, dams, airports, and docks. For living or working space, they design and build homes, offices, and factories. And to those who say that engineers only destroy nature by building things, one can reply that engineers are also involved in preserving wetlands and shorelines, restoring forests, and cleaning up dumps.

Bridges or highways are one way of connecting people; another is the Internet and other communication networks that we depend on today. These networks feature undersea wires, satellites revolving overhead, and wireless communications with microwaves or radio. Electrical, electronics, and communications engineers built every node of these networks.

Engineers not only run factories, they are also developing robots that eliminate boring, repetitive work. They help establish innovative work practices such as self-managed production lines or quality circles—two ways to increase the productivity of workers and the quality of the products. They help develop production techniques that reduce pollution and raise efficiency.

And finally, to those who say that engineers work only in smoky factories or on noisy construction work sites, one could reply that engineers also help artists create new visual forms and musical sounds. They help design new entertainments at amusement parks or video arcades and new sports equipment for the use and enjoyment of the Olympic athlete or the weekend hacker. Engineers are in government, education, charities, and community work. Yes, many engineers work on the factory floor; but many also work in laboratories, offices, on ocean platforms, in the mountains, at the shore, or on city streets.

If there is one dominant message in this book, it is that an engineering education doesn't lead to only one or two types of careers or work environments. Engineering is a gateway to a huge, diverse array of opportunities.

Engineers and Scientists

Many young people who excel in the sciences aren't sure whether a career as an engineer or as a scientist is the best future for them. In many ways, the two careers are similar. Many engineers, especially those who get an advanced degree, do exactly the same type of work as scientists with advanced degrees. They can both work in laboratories, running experiments and analyzing data to develop fundamental rules or principles about how nature works. Conversely, many scientists start their careers in a corporate laboratory or as a quality manager in a production line and then develop into factory managers or administrators.

Some sharp students, having noticed the commonality between the two fields, have decided to study in one field as an undergraduate and in the other as a graduate student. The switch from engineering undergraduate to scientific graduate is somewhat easier than the reverse because engineers take more math than do most science majors. However, it can be done either way.

There are, of course, differences between the two. Most college-level science programs are designed to prepare the student for work in a laboratory or for graduate school. Engineering programs are designed to prepare students for work in business and industry, with opportunities ranging from design to production to sales. This diversity is one of the reasons why there are so many more employment opportunities for engineering students immediately after graduation.

Methods

On another level, the difference between engineering and science is one of philosophy. Scientific work is a search for the truth; engineering work is a search for what is practical. The scientific method, formally defined, is a way to determine the truth or accuracy of a principle by performing experiments that either confirm or deny that principle. Thus, scientific work tends toward conducting lengthy sets of experiments, studying reference materials in libraries, and writing presentations for publication in science journals.

Billy Vaughn Koen, a professor of mechanical engineering at the University of Texas (Austin), has defined the engineering method as:

> The strategy for causing the best change in a poorly understood or uncertain situation within the available resources.

This phrase demonstrates both the power and the limitations of engineering work. Engineers are constantly dealing with uncertainties and often don't have the time or money to obtain an understanding of the scientific principles involved. Thus, engineering work tends toward finding what works for a given situation and then using that solution until another situation arises. Engineering work is a striving for constant improvement. Interestingly, some very basic knowledge of the natural universe has arisen from engineers trying to solve a day-to-day problem. Unexpected results or unusual problems can reveal new insights into physics, chemistry, or other sciences.

Working Conditions

It isn't easy to take abstract principles and understand what work one will be doing in the future. So here's a concrete example from the electronics industry. In the late 1940s three scientists at Bell Laboratories, while trying to establish some new properties of silicon, developed the transistor, a mixture of silicon and germanium. It had such dramatically new properties that a Nobel prize was awarded the researchers, and a new "solid-state" age of electronics began. (Previously, electronic devices were based on vacuum tubes, a complex mixture of glass bulbs, wires, and electric power.)

By comparison, in the mid-1980s a team of engineers at Intel Corporation—the Santa Clara, California, microelectronics producer—was charged with developing the 80486 microprocessor, a circuit chip that would power the next generation of computers. The team had to devise a way to cram 250,000 transistors onto a chip the size of a fingernail, and they had eighteen months to complete it. Almost simultaneously, another team at Intel was being set up to design what came to be known as the Pentium chip, with more than two million transistors, as the replacement for the 486. Each team was aware of the other, but each had different goals and timetables. The 486 team could use one type of materials and fabrication techniques, while the Pentium could use others that were not as well established commercially.

Bell scientists had essentially no timetable to meet because no one was sure whether the things they were trying to accomplish could actually be done. When the scientists made their discovery, they knew that they had developed a fundamentally new way of working with semiconductor materials. They had the satisfaction of knowing that their discovery would eventually change the way electronic equipment was made.

The Intel engineers, on the other hand, had a strict timetable to meet. Their invention (which has generated several patent applications) met predetermined performance goals. They had the satisfaction of knowing that their work would result in sales of new computers and microelectronics for their employer; it would also help the company's customers perform their work more efficiently. But they knew that their product would not live forever because just a few years later, the Pentium chip replaced the 80486 chip.

Most scientists, and nearly all engineers, work in industry. But proportionately more scientists work in academia, teaching, and research. If you are happy in a school environment, there are more opportunities with a science background than with an engineering one. Conversely, an engineering background is more likely to result in a job in industry. It's up to you to decide.

Engineering and Technology

Have you ever helped out in repairing a car, or opened up a radio and tried to take it apart? In figuring out how machines work, you can also figure out how to fix them. Keeping machines running is the fundamental task of technicians, and you may find that your interests lie more in this line of work than in engineering.

What's the difference between these two? Engineers, after all, also help keep machines running. The key difference isn't the type of machine, but in the approach taken to machinery by engineers and technicians.

Technicians, fundamentally, use and repair the machines that engineers develop. A technician will take an existing machine and apply it to some task. Or, the technician may need to discover why a good machine suddenly stops functioning.

A Chemical Factory

In a chemical factory, for example, samples of the chemicals that are being produced are taken out of the production vessels periodically. These samples are sometimes brought to a central laboratory where a technician takes the sample and runs it through an instrument called a chromatograph. This device has the ability to separate chemicals in the sample mixture and measure how much of each chemical the mixture contains. The technician starts up the chromatograph, checks that it is operating properly, puts the sample through, and then analyzes the results. He or she then writes a report describing the components of the mixture and delivers the report to the people running the production process.

An engineer, on the other hand, designed and manufactured the chromatograph. Engineers were also at the chemical factory earlier, when it was built, to help design the process and see that it was constructed properly. Even earlier, engineers were involved in developing the very chemicals that are being produced and in figuring out how to produce them economically. At the present time, one or several engineers are involved in making sure that the process is running as efficiently as it can. It may be an engineer, for instance, who receives the report from the technician and decides that the process must be changed.

This example illustrates how an engineer may set up the tools and equipment for a manufacturing process but leave that process in the hands of technicians to run and maintain. A technician's work can require a high level of sophistication; in some cases, a technician knows more about how to use a machine than the engineer who designed it. Then, too, sometimes the machine is so complex that an engineer is needed to run it. Some machines, especially ones that are newly invented, require complicated tests and analyses even before they perform the intended task.

Maintenance Work

Maintenance work is another way of illustrating the differences between engineers and technicians. Often engineers who are very knowledgeable about a certain type of equipment will know very little about how to maintain that equipment. Computer maintenance, for example, can require a sophisticated understanding of how electronics work and how to solder components together. But many computer engineers work only with blueprints or circuit diagrams and have never held a soldering gun in their hands. However, when a maintenance technician has performed all the tests or repairs he or she knows and a system still doesn't work, an engineering team can be called. A problem that can't easily be repaired may indicate a fundamental flaw in the equipment's design, and the engineers will be best equipped to find it.

Training and Job Opportunities

In terms of training, many technicians are required to take only several months' worth of vocational courses after high school. Many companies, especially those involved in computers, telecommunications, or heavy equipment (airplanes or earthmovers) provide these training courses themselves. The engineer, of course, must have a college degree. There is a middle ground between the engineer who has a four-year degree and the technician with vocational training: a two- or four-year program called engineering technology. This will be dealt with in more detail in Chapter 6, Engineering Technology, but briefly, the engineering technology curriculum provides for more mathematical and scientific training than vocational courses, but with an emphasis on practical knowledge that can be applied almost immediately after graduation.

Depending on the individual, an engineer can often move rapidly into management positions and continue climbing up the corporate ladder. Technicians, on the other hand, have more limited possibilities for promotion.

If you think you have a strong mechanical aptitude, would you prefer operating and maintaining equipment or designing and building equipment? Many people aren't sure. One way to find out is to obtain technical work before or during college. The military offers many opportunities for technician's work, and some of this experience can be transferred directly to a job in the private sector.

Job demand for both types of workers is high today. The engineer tends to have a set of skills that can be transferred from one type of technology to another, while the technician's training is usually specific to one type of machinery or instrumentation.

Engineers and the World

Engineers are the inventors and implementers of technology. It is common to hear that American society—indeed, the world—is becoming more technological. What does this mean?

In a major study published in 1988, the Congressional Office of Technology Assessment (OTA) considered this question. Until it was closed in the 1990s, OTA was a federal agency controlled by the U.S. Congress that examined political issues in a technological context. It regularly issued reports on new technologies in areas such as health care, communications, pollution control, or education. In the 1988 report entitled "Technology and the American Economic Transition," OTA looked at how Americans live and work. It found a complex set of networks, an interconnected web of businesses, economic activities, and people. One example cited goes as follows:

> What could be more basic than frozen pizza? A man cooking a frozen pizza in a microwave oven cares about what the pizza costs, how it tastes, how its preparation fits into his increasingly harried lifestyle . . . Consider a likely chain of events that culminated in the pizza. Knowledge about the health effects of food came from a TV talk

show, and information about a sale on pizza came from a news-paper ad. Wheat for the pizza crust was grown in Kansas using sophisticated seeds and pesticides. The pizza was assembled auto-matically and wrapped in materials that are themselves the prod-uct of considerable research. The pizza was probably purchased at a grocery store where a clerk passed it over a laser scanner, which entered data into a computer and communication system designed to adjust inventories, restock shelves, and reorder prod-ucts. This system in turn made it possible to operate an efficiently dispatched transportation system, placing a premium on timely and safe delivery . . .

The point OTA is making in this example is that even when considering something like food purchased in a supermarket, the marks of technology are all around. Each network on which we depend for our well-being has technological elements. Engineers are actively involved in all of these elements.

The networks OTA analyzed are:

- food
- housing
- health
- transportation
- clothing and personal care
- education
- personal business and communication
- recreation and leisure
- defense
- government activities (besides defense)

If any of these networks surprise you by their presence, read on and you will see how engineering is involved. If you have already targeted one of them as the objective of your career, this book will show you how to get started.

Concern for the Environment

Even though most of these networks represent some type of business, it would be a mistake to believe that all engineers work in business. A good example is concern over the environment. Today's newspaper headlines continually trumpet new environmental worries: acid rain, hazardous waste, workplace safety, global warming, polluted water, and deforestation. There is dramatic debate today over humanity's place in the world and the condition of our planet, which we will pass on to the next generation. Some people believe that the answer is to turn the clock backwards—to reduce the technological complexity of modern life and to live more simply and in better harmony with nature. Others argue that the only answer to the environmental problems caused by technology is more technology. This debate is a philosophical and cultural one and will probably continue for many years to come. In the meantime, however, something has to be done, and engineers are the ones doing it.

Water Treatment

Examples of this work are all around us. Most cities have a water treatment plant to remove wastes before water is discharged to nearby rivers, lakes, or seas. Developing these treatment plants was one of the first activities of civil engineers around the turn of the last century. Today, this technology has advanced to the point where wastewater can be cleaned for reuse—a valuable resource in drought conditions. New filtration technology has also made an age-old goal technically and economically feasible: taking ocean water and removing dissolved salts so that the water is drinkable.

Garbage Disposal

Another example can be seen in garbage disposal. Years ago the disposal practice of most cities was simply to dump it in the closest, most convenient location. Today, however, such landfills are being engineered to have relatively impermeable walls so that the dangerous materials in garbage do not escape into the environment. However, the amount of readily available landfill space is declining, so environmentalists are pursuing efforts to recycle much garbage back into commercially useful materials. Once the suitable materials are found in garbage, they have to be extracted, purified, and reprocessed. Engineers are involved at every step of the process.

Many people have looked at the vast mountains of garbage our society generates and asked why a more effective use and disposal of it wasn't possible. The result has been an increasing reliance on recycling—restoring throwaway items to something of value.

International Opportunities

In a profound sense, engineers are involved in helping sustain people around the world. In underdeveloped nations, the essential elements of life—water, shelter, and transportation—are provided through the efforts of engineers. Advanced technology provides some interesting solutions to tricky problems. For instance, in sub-Saharan Africa, how does one keep pharmaceutical compounds that must be refrigerated? You can't simply put them in a refrigerator because an electric power station may be a thousand miles away. And you may not have the fuel available to run a portable generator. The solution is to use a complex synthetic mineral called zeolite that can use solar energy to provide cooling.

Another example can be seen today in the People's Republic of China where telephones are hard to come by. In Beijing, the capital city, it is common to see officials with cellular telephones, high-tech versions of this essential tool that only in the past decade has become common in the United States. Because underdeveloped countries like China lack the utility infrastructure that has been built up in the United States and Europe, a wireless system such as cellular telephones is more practical. In this way, the business and government community can take advantage of the latest technology, even when the rest of the country is very backward.

Career Options

How about the fun side of engineering? It does exist, even if you aren't aware of it. For example, a booming business today is the construction of amusement parks, which would not be complete without stomach-wrenching roller coasters. These complex machines, as well as many other rides, require extensive structural design work by engineers. You will also find engineers at work in rock-and-roll studios, concert halls, movie sets, sports arenas, and beaches.

Headlines are being captured today by young engineers developing new "multimedia" entertainment, which combines sound, video, and text on a PC screen. Many technology and communications forecasters can envision a day when all types of entertainment are downloaded via fast, broadband channels into the home, creating an instant worldwide market for movies, recordings, and other performances.

Even before all the various engineering specialties have been described in this book, you can see that there are dozens of different engineering functions, job descriptions, and opportunities. It's hard to decide that you want to be an aerospace engineer, a materials engineer, a computer engineer, or whatever. The solution to this problem is simply to make a decision first to be an engineer. Later, you can decide on the specific type.

Selecting a Specialty

There are many reasons, practical and emotional, to delay selecting a specialty. At nearly all college engineering programs, you don't select a major until the end of your freshman year or during your sophomore year. Taking college-level courses as a freshman, talking with faculty and fellow students, and thinking freshly about who you are and where your interests lie, all these things help guide one's decision. There's no need to rush into it now.

A second reason for waiting has to do with the nature of engineering work. Because engineering is a broad profession, there are many different types of work, even within each engineering discipline. Several of the engineering disciplines—especially mechanical, industrial, and electrical engineering—provide entry into nearly every type of manufacturing business, government, research, or other types of organizations. If you are a mechanical engineer, for example, obviously you could work in a field like the automotive industry. But you could also find opportunities in electric utilities, in aerospace firms, in government laboratories, and in other industries.

A third point is that, even within one type of industry, there is great variation in job responsibilities. At factories you could work in design, production, quality control, maintenance, or plant management. At the corporate headquarters, you could work in sales or marketing, business management, administration, or research and development.

A fourth and final point is that over the course of a career, engineers can do many different things. There are engineers who spend their entire career happily in one department of one company, and others who move all around the corporate ladder. There are engineers who start their own companies or who work for themselves, as consultants, and never occupy a company office.

Employment Outlook

There are major differences in career prospects among engineering branches, and the purpose of this book is to point them out to you. At any given time, the job demand varies, depending on the condition of the economy. A look at Table 1.1 illustrates this point. These data, from the latest forecast computed by the U.S. Bureau of Labor Statistics, show the size of various engineering branches as of 2000 and the projected growth through the year 2010. (They do not include every type of engineering degree available, mostly because of technical differences between academic disciplines and job titles; there will be additional information on these unlisted degrees in the rest of this book.)

Table 1.1 Current and Projected Growth of Engineering Fields

Engineering Branch	2000	2010
Aerospace	50,000	57,000
Chemical	33,000	34,400
Civil	232,000	256,000
Computer (hardware)	60,000	75,000
Electrical	288,000	319,000
Mechanical	221,000	250,000

The most important point is to make a commitment to engineering now and choose the specific type of engineering career later. Even in looking at a projection for the year 2010, bear in mind that by that year, you may be five or so years into your career; that leaves another thirty-five years at least to your working life! The key, of course, is to be an engineer—some kind of engineer. The rest is up to you.

Women, Minorities, and Engineering

Special mention deserves to be given to the people who traditionally have been ignored or excluded from the ranks of engineering: women and minority groups. Today, engineering is wide open to minority groups. Many engineers of minority ethnic backgrounds are highly successful and have founded companies worth millions of dollars. Among persons of Asian-Pacific heritage, in fact, proportionately more are engineering students than their fraction in the United States population as a whole. The problem for other minority groups, however, is that there are not enough members in the educational system. The high requirements for a good high school education are an obstacle for some underprivileged inner-city children. The cost of a four-year college education adds to the difficulties.

There has been mixed progress in the entry of women and minority groups into the ranks of working engineers. Female representation across all engineering disciplines has risen slowly but steadily since the 1970s, and women currently represent about 18 percent of graduating engineers. Minority groups (excluding Asian-Pacific members) represent just over 10 percent of recent graduating classes. This proportion appears to be a plateau at the moment.

There are many outreach programs that help sustain minority students in engineering. These include scholarships and intensive training sponsored by the National Action Council for Minorities in Engineering (NACME) and internships and financial support from leading corporations. About fifty thousand non-Asian-Pacific minority engineers have won degrees since 1973. Many more will be needed in the future.

America needs more engineers, and in the face of a smaller number of college-age students of all races in the 1990s, America must get more engineering candidates from women and minority groups. Here is how the Commission on Professionals in Science and Technology, a Washington, D.C., public-interest group, assessed the situation in 1989:

> In science and engineering particularly, [women and minorities] are needed because the nation faces a potential shortfall of considerable magnitude in some of these areas, and white males cannot continue to fill all of the national needs by themselves.

The report, entitled "American Minorities in Science and Engineering," examined the situation of engineers and scientists with Ph.D.s in particular detail. These college graduates will form the core of America's research efforts in the twenty-first century. Today nearly half of all graduate students (master's and Ph.D. levels) are foreign nationals—students from abroad who study here and often return to their homes after graduation. The report notes:

> In 1988, when the size of the age-thirty population was at its peak, . . . American universities awarded doctorates in natural science and engineering to 7,455 American citizens, including 523 (7.2 percent) awarded to minorities. The National Science Foundation projection indicates positions for about 18,000 new Ph.D.s in natural science

and engineering in 2004, when the size of the age-thirty population reaches bottom [around 3.2 million]. Where are they to come from?

The report concludes:

Half of our children are girls. A growing third are members of minority groups, and one sixth are . . . both female and minority. Put another way, only one-third are white, non-Hispanic boys. The world's leading democracy cannot afford to depend on only one-third of its population for leadership in science and medicine, in law and politics, and in all other fields, nor can it afford to have large segments of its youth ignorant of both the facts and processes of science.

Doors are opening wide for women and minority groups in engineering. Career prospects are outstanding. Think hard about yourself and your career aspirations before you pass over the opportunities that engineering represents.

2

THE COMMON ELEMENTS OF ENGINEERING

THIS CHAPTER WILL describe elements that nearly all engineering disciplines share. Most engineers go to school for four years, earning a Bachelor of Science in Engineering (B.S.E.) degree or an engineering technology degree, and then get a job. But some go on to earn a master's degree (M.S.E.), and a few don't stop until they have a doctorate (Ph.D.).

Regardless of the specific degree, engineers can usually find jobs in design, research, technical services, and production. Management opportunities come with experience. Then there are a wide variety of fields from which to choose: manufacturing, construction, agriculture, business services, and government. The pay varies according to degree level, experience, the industry, and, of course, individual performance.

Career Opportunities and Goals

Believe it or not, a great many people who study engineering during college end their careers in a field other than engineering. The reason for this is that over the course of a career, many engineers move into management, or into other lines of work altogether.

This isn't necessarily a bad idea. Each individual, during his or her working career, is usually making choices about whether to continue in an existing job, consider a promotion, or go to another employer. And in many lines of work, having an engineering degree demonstrates strong problem-solving skills that are useful in many other areas. Sometimes, unfortunately, a person finds future career growth stopped simply because there isn't a higher position to move into without leaving engineering work. The point here is that getting an engineering education is a way to open doors to a variety of career opportunities.

One of the first things you should do when considering engineering is to evaluate your long-term goals. You don't have to make a solemn commitment to the goal you choose now. But you should try to get a feeling for whether your long-term preference is research, production, design, or management. This decision will dictate how far you should plan on going in your education and will help guide your choice of engineering disciplines.

Areas of Work

In the following chapters, there will be many details about the specific work in which various engineering specialties engage. Nearly all engineering work, at least early in one's career, falls into one of several categories.

Design

Design is probably the most common type of engineering work. Design simply means taking the knowledge of materials, processes, systems, and nature that one learns in college and adapting it to machines, equipment, structures, production methods, and government regulations. To look at an automobile, for example, is to see the efforts of thousands of design engineers who were instructed to improve a component or part on the basis of new information. It would be intimidating for one person to design each of the thousands of components of an automobile from scratch, although projects as complex as this have been done. More often, there is a large body of existing knowledge about why something was made a particular way. The design engineer becomes familiar with this body of knowledge through experience and then tries to adapt the component or structure to a new situation.

This process may seem dull or uninspiring, but in fact it is one of the most creative and exciting aspects of engineering work. When there is something truly new—a new type of plastic or a new microchip, for example—the engineer must envision how those things will be used. Many of the best engineers consider themselves close to artists because they must envision things that have never existed before.

Production

This is probably the second largest area of work for engineers. Production is simply making whatever product a company is responsible for, as often as desired, and with the level of quality demanded by customers.

In a typical factory, there are many types of equipment doing something to materials or objects as they pass along a line. In a food-processing plant, for instance, grains of wheat can be successively ground to flour, mixed with various ingredients, shaped into cookies, baked, packaged, and shipped. In a steel mill, iron and other metals are melted in a furnace; poured into molds; shaped by rolls into sheets, plates, or bars; treated by heat or chemicals for purity; and put on trucks or railcars to be shipped to another factory. There an equally complex set of steps turns the steel into an appliance part or auto chassis.

Production engineers are responsible for keeping the assembly lines running. This involves an understanding of the product's function and specified quality. In addition the production engineer must know how the various machines that handle the product are operated, so they can be fixed if they break or begin to turn out faulty products. The capabilities of workers must also be taken into consideration. If a machine is being operated incorrectly or inefficiently, that will also affect the final product. Finally the production engineer must keep an eye on the cost of all the production steps. It may be worthwhile to spend a lot of money to improve some step in the production process if the improvement results in lower operating expenses or higher quality.

Production engineering is a fairly direct route to corporate management because no manufacturer can continue to exist if the products it makes are shoddy or cost too much. Production engineers can move from responsibility for one component in a manufacturing process to the entire plant and then to groups of plants.

Construction

Construction, or civil, engineers use many of the same skills as production engineers. One difference is that construction engineers work on buildings, highways, and other permanent structures that are often one of a kind. Like production engineers, construction engineers must understand the final product, the necessary equipment and worker skills, and the economics of the project. Materials of construction are constantly evolving, and so construction engineers must be aware of how these materials are to be used or installed. Construction can, but is not required to, involve outdoor work.

Research

Research done by engineers is often the same thing as research done by scientists. Something is discovered in nature or in the real world, and the engineer or scientist brings that discovery into the laboratory and tries to find out why it occurs.

There is pure research performed by engineers—usually teachers at colleges and universities—that may have no immediate application in the real world. This research is similar to a scientist discovering a new type of star, or a new mathematical equation, and feeling a sense of accomplishment for that discovery. But most research engineers, especially those working for private industry, engage in something called "applied" research. In this case, the engineer is trying to find a way to accomplish a specific objective that his or her employer will then turn into a marketable product or service. For example, a research engineer trying to find out why the turbine blades in jet engines wear out might discover that a different alloy works much better than the alloys currently being used. That discovery is then passed on to other engineers (sometimes called design engineers, sometimes development engineers) who will figure out how to make the turbine blade out of the new material.

Not all research engineers have a doctorate, but many of them do, and having that level of training will open many laboratories' doors. There is also a fairly steady interchange between research and design. At some companies a research engineer will discover a new principle or capability in a laboratory and then follow that discovery in each step through development, design, production, marketing, and sales.

Technical Services and Consulting

Many engineers find lucrative employment by offering nothing more than their judgment, written up in a report, just as a lawyer advises a client to write a contract a certain way, or a doctor advises a patient to follow a certain diet. The product that the consulting engineers sell is their understanding of the technical details of some issue.

For example, many consulting engineers work in some aspect of the construction industry. A client will come to the engineer saying, "We need to reduce traffic jams on our roads." The engineer will observe the situation, analyze the data, think about the underlying problems, and then offer a set of recommendations. The cost of implementing these recommendations is an important element of the final report. In another application, many consultants are being hired today as "systems integrators" for computer networks. A big company will create a list of preferred vendors for the computer system and then turn the list over to the systems integrator. That person or firm will then figure out the best arrangement of components for achieving the customer's goals and provide a report of recommendations. Sometimes, the consultant will oversee the installation.

Technical services and consulting are wide-ranging and very dependent on the entrepreneurial skills of the engineer. Many engineers don't consider a career in consulting or technical services until they have several years' experience in some relevant type of work. Many large corporations, however, employ technical services engineers to help their customers solve problems that might occur in the use of the company's products.

Sales, Marketing, and Product Management

Traditionally engineers have been stereotyped as tongue-tied, shy people who are happier dealing with machines than with other people. That image has been obsolete for a long time, as evidenced by the importance of sales engineering and the marketing and development of commercial technology.

The solitary inventor-engineer still exists today, but more often, invention and product development is the result of collaborative work involving diverse professional teams. Consider, for example, Dean Kamen, who made headlines recently with "It"—the Segway personal-transport device. Kamen, who has 150 patents to his name, formed "a group of talented engineers and designers, dedicated marketing specialists, visionary investors, and committed supply partners" when he formed the Segway Company to develop his invention. (Kamen, who is a member of the illustrious National Academy of Engineering, shares a trait with another technological pioneer, Bill Gates: he is a college dropout. While studying physics, he invented the first of his highly successful biomedical devices.) The point is, carrying an idea from conception to commercialization requires an array of communication skills, and an inventor will either have those skills, or will develop a team that does.

Sales as a career requires good communication skills, the ability to get along with people, persistence, and technical know-how. Technical salespeople need to be able to translate the needs and requirements of the customer into the specifications for the appropriate product. Because this experience is so vital to a manufacturer's success in the marketplace, sales careers often lead to marketing management positions. In many cases the experienced sales engineer will be put in charge of developing a new product and coordinating the campaign to get it out into the marketplace. These product managers are key players in most high-tech companies.

Education

The majority of engineers earn a B.S.E. degree and then go into industry. Undergraduate programs for engineering are accredited by the Accreditation Board for Engineering and Technology (ABET), which periodically reviews the curriculum and teaching facilities of colleges before renewing their accreditation. Many states require that engineers in certain functions (such as public works construction) be graduates of an accredited program.

At the behest of the professional engineering societies, ABET sets the minimum number of specific courses that engineers take. It also specifies such things as laboratory courses, computer programming, and design projects. These courses then become the required curriculum of college engineering departments.

Even though formal study stops for most engineers at the B.S. level, education continues. Most employers have some type of classroom education for new employees. And many engineers find it helpful to take continuing-education courses during their careers to learn about new areas of technology.

About 20 to 30 percent of engineers, depending on the type of discipline they are in, go on to earn a master's degree. Many engineers consider the master's degree the necessary final step for a fully trained engineer. It is quite common for students to take a full-time job and attend night school. Silicon Valley, the area south of San Francisco that is the heart of the electronics industry, came into being, in part, because of the strong base of good engineering schools in the vicinity. These schools served as an anchor for high-tech companies and provided a place where hired engineers could continue their education.

But many engineers can now continue their education in remote locations by gaining access to videotaped courses and computer-networked classes. As you will see in the following pages, many engineering specialties exist primarily at the master's level, so if you want to be fully prepared for working in these areas, the master's program is advisable. Usually M.S.E. graduates can expect to earn annually about $2,000 to $4,000 more than B.S.E. graduates when they start working. But this difference fades over time, as individual performance becomes apparent.

A substantial number of engineering graduates combine the engineering degree with a master's degree in business administration (M.B.A.). The engineering/M.B.A. combination is a powerful one for engineers who expect to move into management or to start their own businesses. So-called "techno-M.B.A.s" have the skills to run businesses, especially those that involve highly technical goods and services. Some schools now offer a "master's in technology" degree, which is tailored for management in highly technical businesses.

The doctorate degree (Ph.D.) is obligatory for engineers who expect to teach at the university level. Many research groups—either in private industry, at federally funded national laboratories, or at research foundations—prefer Ph.D.-level engineers. Annual pay can be $4,000 to $10,000 more than that of a B.S.E. graduate.

A final element in the educational environment is the question of professional licensing. This license is earned by passing two tests and by gaining several years' experience in actual engineering work. Only about 15 percent of all engineers take the time to get this license, and most of these are in the civil engineering profession where government regulations require licensed engineers to review blueprints. Licensure is desirable for any engineers who expect to work as consultants, who hope to start their own businesses, or who plan to spend the bulk of their career in one discipline or area of technology.

Employment in the Private and Public Sectors

According to data on graduating classes, well over one-third of the job offers engineering students receive come from manufacturers. This is no surprise because manufacturing is the sector of the American economy most closely tied to technology.

But this doesn't mean that the remaining sectors of the economy are closed off to engineers. In all likelihood most students head toward manufacturing initially because that's where they find the highest salaries. But there are well-paying jobs in other sectors, and if salary isn't an issue of high importance, practically the entire employment arena is open to the engineering graduate.

Engineers are attractive job seekers because their academic training prepares them to handle numbers easily and to approach work with a positive, problem-solving attitude. The question sets and tests that engineering students take during school are not just a means of getting grades; in many ways, these test questions are comparable to the problems engineers encounter in the real world.

Government service is another significant source of jobs for engineers; the government is perennially short of engineers. The main employment areas in the federal government are the Departments of Defense, Energy, the National Science Foundation (which helps run the network of national laboratories), and agencies such as the Environmental Protection Agency, the Occupational Safety and Health Administration, and the Army Corps of Engineers. The National Security Agency, the Central Intelligence Agency, and the Federal Bureau of Investigation hire large numbers of engineers annually, especially for designing and installing communication networks.

Again, it is important to think about one's long-term career while considering work in any area of the economy. Many engineers perform important work as consultants or business advisers, but they can only do so after gaining experience in manufacturing or government service. In the environmental field, for example, many specialists work first for the federal Environmental Protection Agency, or state-level agencies, and then go on to work for engineering firms that do clean-up projects. Another potential career choice is banking and financial services. Banks need to know as much as possible about the capabilities of the companies for whom they provide loans. Financial firms and stock investors may need advice on the potential of a new technology, the possible results of a shortage of materials or energy, or the effects of a new government regulation.

It is not easy to predict exactly what one would like to do ten or fifteen years down the road. Don't be frustrated if you can't decide now. Make plans to give yourself as many options as you can for the future. If you believe that you might do well in research, plan to take extra science courses. If you think that you might want to be a business manager, take extra economics or business courses, and perhaps make preparations for attending business school after you finish your engineering education.

Engineers and Computers

Computers are something we hear about often; they have entered practically every aspect of business, research, education, and communications. There is a special relationship between computers and engineers. The goal of both is to handle large numbers of data and symbols rapidly and efficiently. Engineers also are the developers of most computer systems, especially the hardware. Today one of the most dynamic elements of engineering is the effort to transform design processes or production methods into computer programs. The effort, when successful, helps engineers tremendously in improving the quality of finished products, and it can reduce the cost of engineering work.

Development of Computers

Ironically, computers weren't always useful to engineers. When computers first became widely available, the time it took to write a useful program, and the cost of the computer itself, made the effort uneconomical. Many engineers also believed that trusting a computer to perform a design function was risky. A small, insignificant mistake in a computer program could make an enormous difference in a final product. There was also the belief that as computers grew more powerful, they would put the engineers who programmed them out of work.

The track record over the past ten years or so has been quite different. As the level of programming experience grew, the programs got better and errors or difficulties were identified. The cost of computers has dropped dramatically. Engineers have found that computers can be a valuable tool to extend their areas of responsibility, so much so that certain types of design work, such as integrated circuits, cannot be performed without them. Today, the business of building computers specifically for engineers—a type of computer called the technical workstation—is a strong market.

Current Trends

The use of computers is having profound implications for many traditional engineering tasks. Many mechanical engineers, for example, must design a part or component that will be cut from metal or molded from plastic. In the past, this design was carried out by making drawings and then performing calculations on the various dimensions of the part. These calculations ensured that the part would hold up under use and that it would fulfill the purpose for which it was designed. When everything checked out, a final drawing was made (again, by hand), and the drawing was taken to the machinists who actually fabricated the part. Now, the design engineer draws the part on a computer screen, then loads a computer program that performs the checks automatically. If a prototype is needed, there are machines that combine computers and fabricators that can form a model from plastic. Finally, another program translates the dimensions into instructions for an automatic cutting or molding machine, and the part can go into production rapidly.

In factory construction an enormously complex set of pipes, girders, vessels, and machines are put in place. Plant design engineers can now put drawings of all the components on a computer screen and then run an "interference check" to make sure that pipes don't cross each other and that they always make the proper connections.

In microelectronic-chip design, some circuits are so complex that they can be planned out only on a computer. Many circuit engineers are experimenting with programs called "silicon compilers" that will automatically create a circuit based on general guidelines that the engineer chooses. The compiler will then arrange the components in a configuration that minimizes the amount of space necessary. All these computer programs are continually being improved, and the confidence level of the engineers who use them is rising.

In the early 1980s ABET made it a requirement for all engineering students to take at least one computer programming course. It would be wise to get additional training, especially through the use of computers in engineering courses. This is becoming easier as more schools acquire access to computing systems. There is no question that the computer will grow in importance in most aspects of engineering work in the future. Today's students should prepare for it.

Salaries and the Intangible Rewards

Here's the good news: at least initially, engineering graduates earn the highest pay of any college graduates. Surveys from such organizations as the National Association of Colleges and Employers show that engineers with B.S. degrees average around $48,000; with M.S. degrees, around $55,000; and with Ph.D. degrees, $65,000 and up. Over the long term, salaries tend to flatten out at a level that is still very high relative to all professionals, but not the highest.

Pay is a sensitive topic for most people. All other things being equal, nearly everyone would like to make more money for the work they do. The trade-off usually involves taking promotions that could require a shift in professional focus—going, for example, from production engineering to plant management, or design to sales and marketing. If higher pay is the sole object, an engineering degree certainly is no hindrance. Some of the highest-paid executives in American corporations started out as engineers.

Not all engineers put the highest priority on the biggest dollars. Many engineers, having gained the experience they believe they need, simply want to continue their current work for the remainder of their careers, getting better and better at that task. For many engineers this means that their pay will begin to level off, with each year's raise less than in preceding years.

Some companies, recognizing the value of such experienced engineers, set up a "dual track" for promotions through the ranks. Under this structure one can move through the ranks in the conventional manner, rising from design or production to management, marketing, or administration. However, one can also rise through another set of positions designed only for engineers and other technical specialists.

The highest pay, at least early in one's career, is with large corporations. The next highest is with small companies, and some of these are on a par with the salaries offered by government. Over the long term, salaries are higher for consulting engineers or engineers who start their own businesses. But with the higher pay go the uncertainties of the job market; one could lose a job if business conditions go sour or get less pay if sales or business goals aren't met.

It used to be true that most engineers, like workers of all types, were hired by a large corporation upon graduation and then spent the rest of their careers with that employer, gradually rising through the ranks. Today the commitment by employers to keep their staff through thick and thin is reduced. For their part most young workers today don't feel exceptionally loyal to their first employer either. The end result is that a certain amount of job-hopping is now the norm. This isn't necessarily bad; many engineers can gain valuable experience by dealing with a technical issue from different sides, for example, as a producer, a user, or a government regulator.

However, you must be ready to manage your career from the outset. Once you have joined a particular company in a particular industry, get familiar with all aspects of that industry. Read business magazines, talk with people in the field, and become knowledgeable about what trends are occurring. At the same time, many engineers benefit by forming strong ties with their professional organization. Join the local section of your engineering society, go to the monthly meetings, and participate in the organization's annual events. The most valuable information about what is going on in an industry comes from talking with fellow engineers about it. Finally, don't rule out getting another job if that job will provide experience that you might value. And if you lose a job, be prepared to win another by having your résumé and other information at the ready.

3

CLASSIC ENGINEERING

THE INDUSTRIAL REVOLUTION wasn't so long ago. If you have elderly grandparents, they may remember listening to a radio station for the first time, or seeing the first of the Model T Fords. And when those grandparents were children, their grandparents could remember the first steam locomotives, the building of the first iron bridges, and the first electric light bulbs.

As the Industrial Revolution arose in Europe in the 1800s, the era of human or animal power transformed to an era of steam power, with engines that could cut wood, move merchandise, or thresh grain. Soon, a steady stream of artisans was coming from Europe to the United States and finding plenty of opportunities to exercise the art of manufacturing. As the century wore on, many new machines were invented in the United States. Soon, with one advance piling on top of another, a complex set of skills called engineering began to be devised. These new skills were taught at selected colleges and universities.

With one exception, it was during those times that the biggest, oldest engineering disciplines formed. The one exception was civil engineering, which used to be called military engineering. Military engineering was the practice of building the roads, bridges, and forts that armies on the move needed. The West Point Academy, founded in 1802, was the source of the first military engineers in the United States. Military engineering began to be taught in 1817. The Rensselaer Polytechnic Institute, founded in 1824, offered the first courses that were formally known as civil engineering.

Each of the engineering disciplines profiled here traces its roots back to the nineteenth century. Even so, an engineer of that era would hardly recognize anything going on in today's versions of these disciplines. Skill in drafting has given way to skill in manipulating images on a computer screen. Familiarity with steam locomotives has been replaced by an understanding of power supplies for communications satellites. Each of the disciplines listed here not only has a long history, but also has a new, up-to-the-minute look.

Electrical/Electronics Engineering

To a large degree, saying that you are an engineer is synonymous with saying that you are an electrical/electronics engineer. The reason for this is the vast number of students studying electronics and the correspondingly large number of such engineers at work today. About one-third of all engineering students are in electrical and/or electronics programs. If computer engineering students and electrical engineering technology students are added together, the number approaches one-half.

Why is electrical/electronics engineering so popular and so dominant among working engineers? Most of the reasons can be found all around you—the radio you might be listening to, the television you might be watching, and perhaps even the computer you might be using. The twentieth century has been called many things, but perhaps the most accurate of all is to call it the Electric Age.

Spurred by new scientific discoveries, and then by practical inventions, electricity has flowed into every aspect of our lives. Electricity supplies light; power to run appliances and heavy machinery; and communications such as the telephone, radio, and television. In much smaller quantities, electricity powers electronics—small devices that mimic large machines. And, of course, electronics is changing everything around us every day, through such pervasive devices as handheld calculators, computers, and control devices that help operate automobiles, airplanes, and homes.

There are roughly 288,000 electrical/electronics engineers at work today, according to federal data. The latest projection from the U.S. Bureau of Labor Statistics is that it will see average growth—11 percent—through 2010, reaching a total of 319,000. Newly graduated B.S.E.E.s earn around $50,000 annually, according to various sources.

Federal data blur the outlook for electrical/electronics engineers somewhat. The U.S. Bureau of Labor Statistics has recently defined a new profession, "computer software engineer," which it characterizes as much involving computer science as it does engineering. (BLS has another category called "computer hardware engineering.") On the academic and professional side, however, there are considerable numbers of electrical engineers whose primary work involves programming computers or similar micro-electronic devices. What makes this more than a trivial distinction is that the Bureau of Labor Statistics projects the current number of computer software engineers as 697,000 and that the growth rate will be an eye-popping 95 percent over this decade, meaning a near-doubling to 1.4 million software engineers. Many of today's B.S.E.E.s will partake of that growth as they find themselves working in various software fields, rather than in hardware. This topic will be discussed in greater detail in the next chapter, where computer engineering will be described.

History

Electrical/electronics engineering has participated in some of the most momentous discoveries in science, both in terms of applying them to practical use and in uncovering phenomena that led to new scientific theories.

The science of electricity had only a rather quaint value as a curiosity for most of history. William Gilbert, an English scientist, characterized magnetism and static electricity around the year 1600, and Alexander Volta discovered that an electric current could be made to flow in 1800. In the mid-1800s a variety of European scientists had established the general rules governing electricity, and, ultimately, theories involving electricity and magnetism were joined under a concept called "electromagnetism" (James Clerk Maxwell's discovery).

Key Inventions

Although the theory largely was developed in Europe, it was in America that most of the first practical applications appeared.

These included the telegraph (Samuel Morse, 1838), the telephone (Alexander Graham Bell, 1876), the light bulb (Thomas Edison, 1878), and the electric motor (Nikola Tesla, 1888). All these inventions—but most of all, Edison's light bulb—soon created the need for systems of generating and conveying electricity and manufacturing the telephones, motors, and bulbs that would use it. The American Institute of Electrical Engineers was formed in 1884, partly to professionalize the growing number of workers in the field and partly to prepare for international visitors expected at the International Electrical Exhibition being held in Philadelphia that year.

From that era to the 1930s, electrical engineering was primarily concerned with figuring out how to generate ever-larger amounts of power and refining the motors, transformers, lighting devices, and other machines that used the electricity. The needs of the electricity industries helped raise the standards of metalworking, machining, and general manufacturing because precisely shaped parts were essential to getting electricity to work correctly. Edison—who went on to create the phonograph (for both recording and playing back), the film camera, and a variety of electrical instruments—brought all his discoveries under the umbrella of the General Electric Company around the turn of the century. Bell's invention, the telephone, led to the creation of American Telephone and Telegraph.

The Birth of Electronics

The triode, a type of vacuum tube developed by Lee De Forest in 1907, and other inventions in England and the United States, led to a variety of devices that could employ a very weak electrical signal. This was the birth of electronics. These inventions helped make radio possible. They were quickly applied to telephony and then, in the 1920s, to commercial radio stations. Along the way, the Institute of Radio Engineers was established in 1912.

The distinction between electricity for power and electricity for communications (electronics) was the cause of some friction in the early years of radio. The overlap in technologies caused the two fields to encroach on each other's territory. Finally, in 1963, the two organizations united to form today's Institute of Electrical and Electronics Engineers, Inc. (IEEE). This division was even more strongly established in Great Britain and Germany, where the fields were identified as "heavy current" (power) engineering and "light current" (electronics) engineering.

Over the years government sponsorship, especially from the military, helped spur the growth of electrical and electronics technology. The early days of radio were boosted by army interest in radio telephones and navy interest in shipboard communications. In World War II, radar and sonar were developed to improve battlefield conditions; these helped spur improvements in electronic components. Federal funding in that era also helped develop the computer. During the 1950s, intensive research was devoted to harnessing atomic energy to generate electricity first for ships and submarines and then for commercial application. And in the 1960s, the young field of space technology and missiles boosted the development of the integrated circuit.

Modern Technology

The integrated circuit—sometimes called the microchip—is a dominant force in electronics technology today. Electronic devices through the 1950s needed a vacuum tube—pieces of metal inside a glass bulb. These tubes tended to be unreliable and to wear out quickly. In 1948 researchers at AT&T invented a solid electronic device, the transistor. This led to a widespread change in electronic designs, which were then called "solid-state." Then, in the early 1960s, researchers at Texas Instruments and Fairchild Semiconductor devised a way to build transistors on a tiny slice of silicon with small wires connecting them. Soon, a way to "write" these circuits on the chip with photographic techniques led to the dramatic situation we have today, with the number of electronic elements on a chip multiplying by the thousands each year.

The computer, primarily an invention of electrical engineers and mathematicians, has shared many of the benefits of the microchip. The basic, modern theories of computing were developed shortly after World War II. The first computers ran on vast arrays of vacuum tubes, with circuits being connected and switched manually. With the transistor, and then the integrated circuit, both the computing action of the computer and the storage of data (the computer memory) were greatly simplified and much less costly. The advent of the computer also led to the development of computer languages. Although it is still very possible to learn computer languages while studying electrical/electronics engineering, a more direct route is usually to study computer science.

The Current Scene

Electrical engineering affects a broad array of manufacturing systems, machines, communications networks, and transportation vehicles. It is hard to think of a machine or appliance without a microchip in it somewhere, and science fiction writers today have fun envisioning a time when we will have microchips implanted in our heads.

The oldest version of electrical engineering, the generation of power, is still a large field, but its size is dwarfed by the other specialties involving electronics. IEEE organizes its membership according to these categories:

- *Division I: Circuits and devices.* This includes microchips, the larger circuits that microchips are wired into, lasers and electrooptics, and related solid-state devices.

- *Division II: Industrial applications.* This covers the manufacturing applications of electronics such as insulation devices, instrumentation and measurement, and electronic devices that control power.

- *Division III: Communications technology.* The fields included here are those most familiar to the general consumer: broadcast electronics, consumer electronics (radios, TV), communication devices (telephones, radio), and radios and similar devices in automobiles.

- *Division IV: Electromagnetics and radiation.* This represents the more advanced realms of communications such as those used for detecting aircraft. Subgroups include antennas and signal propagation, magnetics, microwaves, and nuclear and plasma sciences.

- *Division V and VIII: Computers.* The Computer Society is the single largest division and includes computer hardware and data storage, networks, and electronics for everything from handheld calculators to supercomputers.

- *Division VI: Engineering and the human environment.* Representing the outreach efforts of IEEE, this division includes engineering management, education, professional communication, and the social implications of technology.

• *Division VII: Power engineering.* These are the engineers at utility stations and those who design, construct, and maintain the generators and transmission systems.

• *Division IX: Signals and applications.* More types of advanced electronic transmission and detection are covered here, including acoustics, speech and signal processing, remote sensing, ultrasonics, and aerospace systems.

• *Division X: Systems and control.* Electronics are capable of controlling electrical and mechanical devices, even as electricity provides the power. Robotics, industrial automation systems, information theory, and engineering medicine are some of the subgroups of this division.

Currently, IEEE lists forty-one societies—specialized categories within these divisions. New divisions are formed all the time; some of the most recent include the Council on Superconductivity, the Sensors Council, the Nanotechnology Council, the Neural Networks Society, and the Components, Packaging and Manufacturing Technology Society. IEEE members can join one or several of these societies; each one publishes journals, holds meetings, and creates forums for like-minded engineers to exchange information.

Except for the computer and power engineering societies, the memberships are fairly evenly matched. But wait—there's more. IEEE isn't the only professional society managing the interests of electrical and electronics engineers. There is also the Instrument Society of America (ISA), which has about forty thousand members interested in industrial control and measurement. Not all of the ISA members are electrical/electronics engineers, and some ISA members are also IEEE members. However, the existence of ISA indicates the great number of engineers employed in the electrical/electronics field. There is a Society of Motion Picture and Television Engineers, ten thousand strong, and an equally sized Illuminating Engineering Society of North America. There are at least half a dozen technical associations for computer specialists, with thousands of members (only some of whom have electrical/electronics backgrounds). Thus, the field of interest of electrical/electronics engineers is huge, and there are tens of thousands of them in most of the technical areas.

All engineering disciplines advance new technology, but for the past couple of decades, no discipline has been moving faster than electrical/electronics engineering. This trend will persist for at least the next decade. Computers and semiconductors are continuing to evolve, and the technology for both of these refuses to "settle down" into something predictable and well defined.

Job Titles

With so many avenues of technical development, the list of possible job titles for electrical/electronics engineers is lengthy. Some of the more common ones are as follows:

• *Circuit designer.* Whether it is a microcircuit etched on a silicon chip or a circuit board on a piece of green plastic, these designers apply engineering principles to building circuits that will accomplish the desired objective. Circuit design is one of the most active areas for automated computer design. Many engineers have

written computer programs to figure out the optimum arrangement of circuit elements.

• *Communications engineer.* Most of the many mass-market, long-
distance communication networks—such as telephones, radio, television, and cable television—rely on these engineers to develop the
best ways to send and receive the communications signal. Signal
fidelity and immunity to electronic "noise" are constant goals.

• *Computer engineer.* The design and construction of computers is one of the more prominent occupations of electrical engineers. These engineers must, of course, be familiar with circuits
and microchips, but they must also have more than a passing
knowledge of computer programming. For this reason many engineers interested in computer design major in that field (computer
engineering), which offers more programming course work.
(Employers appear to be evenhanded when choosing between the
two specialties; the real distinction is the student's own course
work and interests.)

Once a design has been completed and a prototype built, highly
sophisticated tests are run to make sure that the computer can perform as expected. Usually problems are encountered that necessi-
tate redesign. Similarly, each computer coming off the production
line is tested for reliability and performance.

• *Control engineer.* The ability of computers and electronic
devices to provide automatic control of appliances, machines, and
manufacturing processes is generating high job demand for these
specialists. One of the most dramatic possibilities is the use of artificial intelligence computer programming to make processes "think."

• *Robotics engineer.* Robotics suffered a downturn in business growth during the 1980s from which it is still recovering. But the long-term future is still bright. Robotics and control engineers share many of the same goals.

• *Power systems engineer.* The design and operation of modern utility plants is extremely complex, more so when nuclear energy is involved. A widening gap between the capacity of newly built power plants and the demand for electricity is expected to generate high job growth for power engineers.

Of course, many other electrical/electronics engineers are involved in testing, maintenance, production, research, and other types of engineering work.

A Control Engineer

Jane has an exciting entry to professional work, an involvement in a first-of-its-kind artificial intelligence program to automate a common manufacturing process—water treatment. Just as water in an automobile's radiator helps keep the motor running, factories, power plants, and other facilities need to circulate cooling and heating water. This process water must be treated continuously to prevent corrosion and scale buildup inside the circulation pipes and pumps. Jane's company, a contract supplier of water treatment systems, wants to replace the constant attention to water conditions that requires several workers with a control computer that would inject the right mix of anticorrosion chemicals at the right time. It's heady work for an electrical engineer who just finished her master's degree.

One of the reasons Jane took this job was that there were few electrical engineers at the company and no one in her specialty—

artificial intelligence. This gives Jane the chance to work on totally new systems; at the same time, it puts a spotlight on her that, if she were to fail, would be painfully bright.

The system Jane has designed marries a new semiconductor chip with an off-the-shelf personal computer. This PC is connected to standard industrial sensors and controllers that make chemical analyses of the process water and then open or shut the appropriate valves and start or stop pumps. The chip and PC have all the "intelligence" needed to compute appropriate control actions, but Jane needs to determine the exact goals of the system so that the right instructions can be programmed into the PC.

To do this Jane engages in what is called "expert systems development." She interviews several senior engineers who have either a chemical or mechanical engineering background. She finds out that the chemicals change the acidity of the water, causing dissolved salts to precipitate out before the process water runs through the system. She figures out the chemistry of the process and how valves and pumps are made to operate. Both of these areas send her back to her college textbooks to freshen up her understanding of chemistry and mechanics.

Finally all the instructions are fed into the computer, and laboratory test runs show the system responds correctly. The system will now be field-tested at a customer's site, and Jane will monitor that work for most of the rest of the year to make sure the system works right.

An Aerospace Electronics Engineer

The general term for electronics on aircraft is "avionics," and Raul likes to think of himself as an avionics engineer. He is part of a group of twelve engineers in a section of fifty avionics engineers, all of whom work for a major defense contractor. The fifty engineers are responsible for all the avionics for a new fighter jet the contractor is designing for the air force.

This project was unusual in aerospace industry practice because it involved competition among three defense contractors. Eighteen months ago, after submitting designs to the air force, each firm was given a sum of money, and had to invest money of its own, to build a prototype of the aircraft. The three prototypes were then tested competitively, and the winner was selected. Raul's firm won.

Now his team is involved in detailing the electronic subsystems that were only outlined during the competition. As is often the case, the electronic technology has changed drastically from the time when the original design was written until the new design must be prepared. In this case, chips made of gallium arsenide are superseding silicon chips for a microwave receiver. The subcontracting firm that is building the circuit boards wants to switch to the new chips, but they are more expensive. Raul must decide whether to go along with the subcontractor's wish, insist on the existing design, or propose something different.

After reading the new chip's performance criteria closely, Raul realizes that there is a trade-off: the new chip is more expensive, but it can perform better. In fact, using the new chip will simplify elements of another circuit that feeds signals into the board he is concerned with. He checks with the group members responsible for this circuit and finds that they are willing to change their design to suit his.

After several discussions, they arrive at preliminary cost figures (more for the new chip, less for the other circuit board) and find that the costs roughly balance out. Because the gallium arsenide chip is more reliable, overall opinion tilts strongly in favor of making the switch. Raul now begins to prepare a report for his group leader. This report will become part of another report that the group leader will send to the company's upper management, and eventually to the Defense Department for review.

Education

Electrical/electronics engineering can be one of the most mathematical types of engineering. Whereas most other engineers are limited by the materials they use (concrete for bridges, steel for boilers), electrical/electronics engineers can work with circuits made of a great variety of materials, which can achieve a wide range of effects. Students of this field aren't required to take more math courses than most other engineers, but many of them do in order to improve their proficiency.

Another distinction of the electrical/electronics field is that many baccalaureate graduates go on for a master's degree—often earning it at night while working full-time during the day. The rapid pace of change in electronic technology makes it important to keep up, and one of the better ways of doing this is extending one's study. The IEEE figures show that about one out of three electrical/electronics engineers earns a master's degree.

The typical courses for an undergraduate, beyond the normal requirements for all engineering students, follow two tracks: one for electrical and computer engineering and one for computer science/computer engineering. Course topics for electrical/computer engineers include:

- electromagnetic fields
- circuit design

- logic circuits
- computer architecture
- energy conversion

For the computer science/computer engineering major, the courses include more computer programming:

- computer hardware
- software engineering
- operating systems
- communications

A wide variety of technical electives exist in the many specialty areas of electrical/electronics engineering.

Mechanical Engineering

Mechanical engineering is machines. Machines, power systems, factory production lines, computers, boilers, and pressure vessels are part of the mechanical engineering scene. The most obvious area of employment for mechanical engineers is the automotive industry, but fewer than 5 percent of all mechanical engineers work in that field. Companies that produce aircraft or electrical machinery, power utilities, and the federal government are other key employers.

Mechanical engineering is the third-largest engineering profession (behind electrical and civil); there are 221,000 mechanical engineers at work today, and the projection is for average growth to 250,000 by the year 2010, according to federal data. Newly graduated B.S.M.E.s earn roughly $48,000.

History

Mechanical engineering can trace its roots back to the very beginnings of the Industrial Revolution, from 1750 to 1800 in Europe and 1800 to 1850 in the United States. Perhaps the most important single invention prior to the actual creation of the profession was the steam engine, invented by James Watt in 1802. In short order this led to the steam locomotive and self-propelled boat. These two modes of transportation soon caused canals and railroad tracks to appear all over Europe and then in the United States. Somewhat later, the adaptation of the steam engine allowed the mechanization of agriculture to begin. It freed manufacturing plants from water power, which had been the traditional source of power for running conveyors and grinding and cutting machines.

The American Society of Mechanical Engineers was founded in 1888 by a group of leading businesspeople and the editors of a magazine called *American Machinist*. Two more developments created new demand for mechanical engineers around that time. One was the automobile, powered by the combustion of oil or other fuel. The other was the application of electricity for lighting—one of the many discoveries that came out of Thomas Edison's laboratories in the 1800s. With an electrical lighting system for the home or for city streets came the need for power generators and electrical conveying equipment. And with the automobile, the need for precisely machined metal became critical, as well as a more formalized method of assembling the components into finished autos.

Twentieth-Century Developments

By the 1920s, with the addition of the airplane to the growing number of methods of transportation, social commentators were hailing the establishment of a "machine civilization." The excitement of that time matches the excitement being generated today by computers.

Also by this time, the central element of mechanical engineering began to be clarified: the generation and use of power. Power means automotive horsepower, the watt-hours an electric utility generates, the thermal units that a heating system produces, and the thrust of a space rocket. Taking some form of energy and converting it into useful work is the primary activity of mechanical engineers.

A good example of this idea and of how mechanical engineers work can be found in a unique publication sponsored by the American Society of Mechanical Engineers (ASME). That publication is the *ASME Boiler and Pressure Vessel Code*. The 2001 edition (the seventy-ninth) runs sixteen thousand pages! Luckily, it is now available on a single computer-compatible CD-ROM disk. The *Boiler and Pressure Vessel Code* provides all the details on how to design, assemble, and test a tank, usually made of steel, that contains heated water or high-pressure steam. The rules of the *Code* are written into state and national safety standards, and because they are followed with great exactitude by mechanical engineers, there are relatively few boiler explosions today. These explosions were a common occurrence in the 1800s on steamships, railroad trains, and in heaters and power systems.

During World War II the concepts of mechanical engineering were very important to the design of aircraft, tanks, and ships. This period also saw the first joining together of mechanical devices with electronics. In fact, the first computers, which were very mechanical devices, were developed by military-funded projects aimed at developing a way to compute the firing trajectories of artillery shells. World War II also brought about the development of the space rocket and the jet engine, which are commonplace today.

The mating of electronics and computers also made automatic machines—robots—possible. This field, expected to become a fast-growing, gigantic business a few years ago, is quieter right now. But most forecasters expect that as the cost and difficulty of guiding machines by computer become reduced, robotics will become a key technology in the future.

The Current Scene

As one of the largest engineering professions, with employment opportunities across most types of manufacturing, the mechanical engineering profession is subject to the same ups and downs as the United States economy as a whole. The economy has been performing well for most of the past decade, and the forecast is for continued, if slightly slower, growth in the future.

In the 1970s, as energy prices skyrocketed, the mechanical engineering profession became one of the most prominent in the effort to conserve energy and make energy-intensive processes and machines more efficient. This need to conserve energy led to the implementation of minimum mile-per-gallon ratings for automobiles and energy-efficiency ratings on household appliances, among other applications. A tremendous amount of work was performed by mechanical engineers in redesigning all these machines.

Today, with energy prices mostly stable, energy efficiency is a less critical factor. What has come to the fore now is the need for less pollution. Exhaust gases from cars, aircraft, power plants, and heating systems have caused air pollution, acid rain, and the decrease in the ozone layer of the earth's atmosphere (which protects us from harmful solar radiation). The most profound problem, however, is the warming of the planet, caused by an increase in the amount of carbon dioxide gas in the atmosphere. Although still subject to much research and debate, a number of scientific analyses point to this gas as the cause of the "greenhouse effect" in which heat and radiation enter the earth (mostly from the sun), but cannot escape through the thickening blanket of carbon dioxide in the atmosphere.

The global warming issue is troublesome because when something is burned or ignited, carbon dioxide gas is almost always generated. Striking a match, lighting a wood fire, or even breathing produces carbon dioxide. To reduce the amount of combustion in the civilized world will require enormous changes in how we do things. Mechanical engineers will be at the forefront of contending with this issue in the future.

New machines are appearing all the time, including more advanced robots. In the past, a mechanical engineer used to sit at a drafting table figuring out the dimensions of the parts of a piece of equipment. Then a machine shop cut and ground the metal to form prototypes of the parts. Today much of this design work is done with specialized computer programs called CAD (computer-aided design). The vision of the future—which mechanical engineers are gradually turning into a reality—is to develop designs on a computer, test them with other programs, then send the designs to automated production machinery that will fabricate and assemble the parts. This procedure will make possible very fast redesigns to meet customer demands and lower production costs.

To give an idea of the many types of work mechanical engineers do, take a look at the following list. These groups are the divisions or special interest areas of the members of the American Society of Mechanical Engineers.

- *Basic engineering*, including fluids, applied mechanics, heat transfer, tribology (the study of lubrication), and bioengineering
- *General engineering*, covering management, safety, and technology and society
- *Manufacturing*, involving materials handling, production engineering, textile engineering, process industries, and plant engineering and maintenance
- *Energy conversion*, including fuels and combustion technologies, internal combustion engines, power and nuclear engineering
- *Materials and structures*, comprising materials, pressure vessels and piping, nondestructive evaluation engineering (i.e., testing materials without destroying them), offshore mechanics, and arctic engineering
- *Energy resources*, involving petroleum, solar energy, ocean engineering, and advanced energy systems
- *Environment and transportation*, covering the topics of rail, aerospace, environmental control, solid-waste processing, noise control, and acoustics
- *Systems and design*, comprising dynamic systems and control, design engineering, computers in engineering, electrical and electronic packaging, and fluid power systems and technology

This list also gives one a sense of the job titles available, ranging from design to production, testing, or computer analysis.

Mechanical engineers can spend all their time writing computer software or work full-time on a factory floor. Many mechanical engineers also ascend to corporate management. The range of opportunities is very broad.

Job Titles

Wherever there are machines, there are mechanical engineers. Of course, a higher concentration of engineers are in the areas of industry where machines are produced—automotive, aircraft, machine tools, and power generation systems. Some of the typical job titles are:

- *Design engineer.* These engineers work with computer programs, laboratory models, and prototypes to develop new machinery or components. Today many types of machines are developed with electronic components. The electronics provide control and measurement capability, and the mechanical devices transform the electronic instructions into physical action. Thus, knowledge of electronics and control theory is helpful.

- *Manufacturing/production engineer.* The 1990s were characterized by an enormous adjustment to robotics and computer controls in manufacturing processes. The concept of "supply chain management"—overseeing the flow of raw materials or components into a factory, through the production lines, and out to inventory or to the customer's site—became the driving force of assembly-type manufacturing. Higher quality and faster throughputs—all at lower costs—remain the challenge. Mechanical engineers with this kind of experience can move rapidly into corporate management.

• *Maintenance engineer.* Keeping production lines, power plants, and other machinery running smoothly is an essential part of manufacturing. Maintenance engineers work with mechanics and technicians to get a balky machine back into operation; the difference is that the mechanical engineer also looks at why a machine is failing. Is it too old and needs replacement? Is there a design flaw? Is it being used incorrectly on the production line? Answering these questions requires sophisticated analysis of the problem.

• *Power engineer.* Some power engineers have an electrical engineering background, but most of the others have a mechanical engineering degree. In many applications, including electrical utilities, generating stations, and aircraft companies, the actual power-production machine is a turbine generator or can sometimes be an internal-combustion engine. Mechanical engineers have a strong understanding of both.

• *Automotive engineer.* As with the power engineer, many, but not all, automotive engineers have a mechanical degree. They can also be electrical, chemical, or industrial engineers, among others. Automotive engineers have their own professional organization— the Society of Automotive Engineers. (See Appendix B.) They work in design, production, and testing for automakers and their suppliers.

• *Reliability and testing engineer.* Long-term performance is a key characteristic of well-built machines. These engineers develop testing methods and review processes to determine how well equipment stands up to use.

A City Planner

Shirley works for an urban planning/technology group that does contract work for governments. Her firm has a contract with one of the California air-quality districts that oversees environmental issues on a regional basis within California. Shirley's firm will help develop a future air pollution–reduction plan for the district. The issue she has to decide today is how to apportion essential services, which may involve pollution-generating machines or systems, while reducing overall pollution levels.

The region her firm is examining has a mix of power companies, agriculture, light and heavy manufacturing, and mass transit systems. Of course, there are also many people with homes that have heaters and cars that have exhaust pipes. Conceivably, she could write a proposal to ban all private ownership of automobiles and let industry grow much larger. She could also mandate the shutdown of all heavy industry and let people enjoy as many cars as they want.

Obviously, both these cases are extremes that could not be put into effect. Some set of conditions between the two must be established. Shirley applies her knowledge of trends in the technology of power generation and automotive technology to the issue of pollution generation. She knows that if a number of programs for low-polluting alternative fuels are established, automotive pollution could be reduced. She begins checking with other engineers in the transportation business to find out about other options.

The contract will go on for several months, and after that, public debate over the various options will begin. Shirley knows that this knotty issue won't be solved any time soon, but she also knows that facing it is inevitable. Something will have to be done about air pollution in this region, and the planning had better start now.

A Production Engineer

Aaron is a plant engineer at a paper mill, but at this time he considers himself to be a high-class mechanic. The machine he is running is an enormous wood chipper—a machine that has rotating shafts powered by electric motors. It cuts logs of Georgia pine into small chips, which are then treated with steam and chemicals to produce the pulp out of which paper can be made. This chipping machine is a new addition to the plant; the previous chipper was retired after a decade of service. For the past three months, Aaron has been monitoring the machine's performance on an hourly basis.

He takes a personal interest in the machine because he had a say in deciding what vendor would supply the machine and in writing the specifications upon which it was assembled. A new feature of the machine is the use of what are called adjustable-frequency drives. This technology, being adopted by many different industries in many applications, has only recently been examined for wood chippers. Aaron argued strongly for its use because it offers the potential of reducing electricity consumption in the chipper. And electricity prices, while relatively low in some parts of the country, have been rising steadily. The machine will earn its cost several times over if the power consumption drops as planned.

The problem right now, though, is that power consumption is still relatively high. Aaron has been taking measurements of the "load" (the amount of force being applied) to each of the motors that drive the rotating shafts. He thinks he has located the problem. Each motor is supposed to run independently, adjusting its output as logs of varying lengths and shapes enter the chipping section. But because of the way the power controls on the motors have been specified, one motor controller is dictating the speed at which all the other motors are running. Some of them are thus running faster than necessary.

To prove this theory, Aaron uses a downtime period to rewrite the software that runs the controllers. This software isn't a computer program. Rather, it is simplified instructions that are used by a device called a programmable-logic controller (PLC), which in turn manages the frequency controllers on each motor. Aaron can do this rewriting at a personal computer in his office, debug the instructions, and then transfer them to the PLC on the chipper. Aaron does so and finds that power consumption is dropping nicely once the chipper begins operating again. The situation will still have to be monitored, however.

Education

Mechanical engineers take the same chemistry, physics, and math courses that most other engineers are required to have during their freshman and sophomore years. In addition there are specialized courses for mechanical engineering, including:

- statics, dynamics, and kinematics—the study of how motion is propagated by structures
- control theory—how mechanical motion can be started or stopped by control devices
- thermodynamics
- mechanical design
- computer systems
- metallurgy

About one out of three ASME members has a master's degree (M.B.A. and/or engineering).

Civil Engineering

To build may be a primal urge. Our constructions, while they may be simply for shelter or transportation, often include aesthetic touches that are there to make us feel good about what we have built. Thus, bridges have geometrical designs intended to support weight, but they also have an artistic detailing and a "look" that defines the era in which they were built.

In constructing buildings, highways, and bridges, civil engineers work with architects to develop the appearance of the structure. Ugly buildings represent a failed communication between the two professionals; a building that falls down, or cannot be maintained, represents an equivalent failure, but one that the civil engineer should have prevented.

But civil engineering is much more than erecting skyscrapers or bridges. Civil engineers are trained in the interactions among structures, the earth, and water, with applications ranging from highways to dams and water reservoirs. Involved in the process of specifying appropriate construction materials, many civil engineers are also employed by the manufacturers of those materials. And, since constructing a large building or public works project can involve elaborate planning, civil engineers can be outstanding project managers. They sometimes oversee thousands of workers and develop advanced computerization and planning policies.

Most significantly, many civil engineers are involved with preserving, protecting, or restoring the environment. Most water treatment and water purification projects are designed and constructed by civil engineers (in these two areas, many of them are known as sanitary engineers). A growing number of civil engineers are involved in billion-dollar projects to clean up toxic industrial or municipal wastes at abandoned dumpsites. Civil engineers engage in such diverse projects as preserving wetlands or beaches, maintaining national forest parks, and restoring the land around mines, oil wells, or factories.

There are about 232,000 civil engineers at work today, according to federal data. This total is expected to rise by approximately 10 percent—an average rate—reaching 256,000 by the 2010. Current salaries are about $42,000 for new graduates.

History

Construction is one of humanity's earliest organized activities. Therefore, it is no accident that civil engineering was one of the very first to be formally set up (in the early 1700s in France). In the United States, the American Society of Civil Engineers (ASCE) was organized in 1852. It was the first national engineering society in the country.

In the mid-1800s and through to this day, one of the central tasks of civil engineers was the design of roads and bridges. The history of American technology can be traced in the bridges around the country, with wood being replaced by iron and steel. Then, in such landmark structures as the Brooklyn Bridge (completed in 1883), beams or girders were replaced by steel cables. In this century new forms of concrete and steel-reinforced concrete are the most common bridge-building materials. The advent of the automobile set off an avalanche of highway construction, culminating in the legislation that set up a national highway trust fund in the 1950s. Since then, thousands of miles of interstate highways have been built, redefining the landscape of America and its cities.

The "civil" in civil engineering refers to the discipline's involvement in public works including government buildings, housing, water treatment works, mass transit systems, airports, shipping ports, and parks. Because of this involvement, many civil engineers find themselves employees of, or suppliers for, local government. This relationship, combined with the requirements for public safety, translates into a high degree of professionalism. Civil engineers with professional engineer (P.E.) licenses are fairly common, and if a civil engineer expects to perform publicly funded work, getting the P.E. license should be a priority.

The computer has had a significant impact on the civil engineering profession. The traditional stereotype of a civil engineer is one who is carrying around a large set of blueprints of the details of a structure. Large staffs of draftspeople working with precise mechanical pencils and rulers would have generated the blueprints. Today most of that work is done on high-powered, graphics-rich computer workstations. As the designer adds components, the computer keeps track of their location and can generate accurate drawings from any perspective. "Bills of materials"—the list of types and quantities of construction materials—are added up automatically. The most advanced workstations allow the viewer to "walk through" a computer-generated animation of what the yet-to-be-built structure will look like.

A key word that arose in the 1980s and will remain important for civil engineers for many years to come is "infrastructure." This term refers to the facilities that local, state, and federal governments provide in order for private industry to expand, or for improving the services for private citizens.

The Current Scene

Construction is a key part of the overall American economy. Data from the U.S. Department of Commerce show that more than

$568 billion are spent each year on new construction and billions more on repair and maintenance of existing structures. To this half-trillion-dollar total can be added the $168 billion or so that is paid for construction materials. Many civil engineers specialize in the development and production of new construction materials.

Infrastructure demands will remain a key part of the civil engineering scene for years to come. With most of the interstate highway system in place, there is now a need for maintaining it and for adapting it to new traffic patterns. Similarly, the nation's airports, railroads, and waterways need regular refurbishing. The housing stock of private homes, apartment buildings, and facilities like colleges or hospitals get renewed on a steady basis.

Civil engineering also comes to the fore when social changes foster new development. In the 1950s and 1960s, much business growth was created by the construction of the interstate highway system. In the 1970s the prominence of the Sunbelt became apparent; northern states have been losing population, while southern and western states have gained dramatically. Such population swings require new construction for roads, schools, water systems, and housing.

Overall, however, the civil engineering field in the United States is not as dynamic as it was two or three decades ago when the interstate highways were being constructed, when new communities were popping up all over the land, and when public funds were more available. The United States economy was also growing at a faster clip during the 1950s and 1960s, resulting in a higher demand for new factories. Today the reduced demand for civil engineers can be seen in the slightly lower salaries that civil engineers earn coming out of school. Most salary surveys indicate that

B.S.C.E.s get 10 to 20 percent less than other engineering majors. It is still, however, a very healthy salary.

This is not to say that one cannot have a wildly successful career—and make lots of money—in civil engineering. Perhaps more than in most engineering professions, civil engineers work as partners in privately held firms. These firms are set up the same way a law firm is, with several senior partners sharing the profits and junior partners and associates earning salaries until they move up to senior status.

The business is what you can make of it. At the same time, saying that there is less growth in the American economy is not the same as saying there is no growth. New factories are being built, new skyscrapers and bridges are going up across the land, and more environmental work is being scheduled.

Job Titles

Over the past couple of decades, the broad field of civil engineering has become specialized in a number of areas. Civil engineers with one type of experience are able to shift to another area, but the real career growth occurs as one becomes an expert in one of these specialties:

• *Structural engineer.* This is the classic civil engineer, concerned with designing walls, towers, bridge spans, dams, or foundations. A knowledge of construction materials and methods is combined with analytical techniques that determine how much weight or mass a structure is carrying, what forces it must withstand (such as wind or water), and, in cases where an architect is involved, how best to accomplish the architect's vision.

• *Construction engineer.* This engineer works at the construction site transforming blueprints and drawings into cement and steel reality. Besides understanding the principles by which a structure was designed, the construction engineer must manage the actual work. This can involve elaborate scheduling and planning so that materials and workers are brought to the site and complete their purpose in the proper order. Time pressure and an awareness of the financial elements of a project are constant objectives. Because the work is done outdoors, sometimes in very remote areas, one must be prepared for a lifestyle of "camping out" in temporary quarters for long stretches of time.

• *Surveying and mapping engineer.* Even before a design is worked out, and as construction begins, teams of surveying and mapping engineers are at work. They use electronic instruments and even satellites (which provide detailed overhead views) to measure the dimensions of the project. Some construction projects can cover dozens of square miles of territory. Elevations must be determined and calculations made regarding how much earth needs to be moved.

• *Transportation engineer.* Do you prefer to travel by plane, train, auto, or bus? Transportation engineering has provided the wealth of traveling options we enjoy today. Highway design is constantly being improved by making roads safer and, in urban areas, making plans for handling increased traffic. Transportation engineers also oversee the design and construction of mass transit systems such as subways, which require tunneling; railway construction; and research on commuting plans.

A subspecialty within transportation engineering is the pipeline engineer, who determines the movement of water, oil, or gas through pipelines. In certain aspects this field is comparable to highway design, with the distinction that a liquid is being conveyed, rather than vehicles.

• *Environmental (sanitary) engineer.* These engineers specialize in water and wastewater projects, land remediation, aqueducts, and garbage disposal. This field is currently one of the fastest growing of all engineering specialties; billions of dollars are being allocated for water and wastewater treatment and for methods of processing garbage and other solid wastes.

• *Hydraulic and irrigation engineer.* Utility companies and many factories, farms, and river or lake barges depend on a steady source of water. These engineers perform the planning, design, construction, and maintenance to keep those water supplies available. Dam design and construction, flood control, and the design and construction of reservoirs, wells, and aqueducts are all common projects. It used to be that hydraulic engineers were concerned with draining swamps and straightening waterways. These days, they are as likely to be constructing swamps and estuaries to preserve the environment and provide reserves for fish and wildlife.

• *Geotechnical engineer.* Along with geological engineers, these engineers help determine the underlying rock strata that affect roadways, water reservoirs, bridges, and other large structures. Earthquake planning and preparation also fall into this category.

A Surveying Engineer

John is feeling more relaxed these days, realizing that a major contract his new firm undertook is now winding down. As one of the founding partners in the firm, he has had several anxious months in the past couple of years as the firm waited for business to come in. But now, on the verge of completing its biggest project to date, he can breathe a little easier.

John's firm specializes in site preparation work. They do surveys to determine the size and shape of the terrain at a project site, as well as underground probes to find where bedrock and underground streams might lie. Together, these tasks must be performed in order to figure out where bulldozers must cut or where explosives must be used to move rock strata.

A new hospital is being built, over several hundred acres, in a rather remote corner at the end of a valley; the remoteness is expected to add to the restful feeling for patients and visitors to the hospital. The general contractor—the firm that will be responsible for the overall project—gave John's firm a contract to do the site preparation. John was the overall supervisor for his firm's work.

The first step was a survey, which involved carrying electronic surveying equipment up and down the hills on the site. John also hired a photogrammetry expert to take aerial photographs and to convert those to dimensional drawings of the site elevations. John spent a good part of the previous spring hiking with the surveying crew, but his main responsibility was to monitor their progress, not to do the actual surveying.

The next step was to bring a well-drilling crew out to the site, not to dig wells, but to take core samples of the ground. John monitored this work closely, having specified where the crew was to dig. He also had a hand in analyzing the core samples as they were delivered from the site. The workers found a couple of underground streams—not unexpected in terrain such as this—and one big surprise. A low-lying area in one corner of the site had apparently been used before as a dump by a company that burned coal. The workers found samples of ash that were identifiable as coal wastes, as well as a heavy concentration of coal tars. The general contractor, and the hospital management firm, were extremely interested in these results because new federal and state laws dictate that the landowner must clean up any harmful waste products found at a site.

John's firm helped characterize the size and composition of the waste materials, which were under a dozen feet of soil. Chemical laboratory tests showed what types of waste products were at the site, and John was able to verify that the wastes would have to be removed.

As John began finishing up the final report of the site preparation survey, he was proud of his firm's professionalism. They handled all the details of the surveying, provided the guidelines for where earth had to be moved, and saved the owner from a big problem by finding the dumpsite before construction began. John expects that this project will lead to more contracts with other general contractors.

Education

In addition to the core courses that nearly all engineering students attend, civil engineers choose from an extensive list of civil engineering classes. Some students make selections based on the specialty they desire to follow; others, not having any specialty in mind, try to fit in as many of the civil engineering courses as possible. The list of civil engineering courses includes:

- surveying and design graphics
- materials design and specification
- geology and hydraulics
- structural analysis
- soil mechanics
- sanitation engineering
- transportation engineering
- geology
- environmental engineering
- oceanography
- steel and/or concrete structures

About a third of the students earning a B.S. degree go on to take a master's, in which specialization in one of the civil engineering programs is intensified. In addition, a proportionately higher number of civil engineering students take the time to qualify for a professional engineer's (P.E.) license. As stated above, this license is often a requirement for being involved in public works or for buildings, so many civil engineers need the license to practice.

Chemical Engineering

Chemical engineering takes the knowledge that chemists obtain in laboratories and tries to turn it into tonnage quantities of materials for social needs. Not all the materials are provided by the ton, or even by the pound. The latest biocompounds coming out of genetic engineering laboratories are extracted and purified via chemical engineering technology; some of them are worth more than $25,000 an ounce. Pure gold is cheap by comparison.

There are about 33,000 chemical engineers at work today. The Bureau of Labor Statistics projects that this number will increase by some 4 percent, to about 34,400, by 2010. Newly graduated B.S.Ch.E.s win salary offers of around $52,000, according to various surveys.

History

During the period 1850–1900, a variety of industries grew in importance in the United States. The new products included paper, fertilizers, refined metals (as the mineral-rich American West opened up), and energy products including coal and, later, petroleum. The industry where the most chemistry knowledge was applied was in textile dyeing, and most of the technology for this field came from Germany.

Industry got by with a combination of chemists (often called "industrial" or "applied" chemists) and mechanical engineers. The chemists devised the reactions that produced valuable products, and the mechanical engineers devised the vessels and equipment that carried out these reactions.

Rising Professionalism

By the turn of the century, the needs of industry for mechanical engineers with specific training in chemical processes led to the establishment of a number of chemical engineering programs. The very first, by most accounts, was at the Massachusetts Institute of Technology in 1888. There was some resistance to the establishment of these programs by chemists' professional organizations, but by and large the needs of industry overcame this resistance.

In 1908 there were a sufficient number of well-established chemical engineers that they could consider starting an organization of their own. The American Institute of Chemical Engineers came into being in that year in Philadelphia.

The profession grew gradually during the 1900–1920 period, until the end of World War I. One of the outcomes of that war was the embargo of many critical materials from Germany, which necessitated a scramble in the United States to set up production of these materials. Many German-owned companies were also expropriated as a means of reparation for the cost of the war. These companies needed United States citizens for management.

Unit Operations

After World War I, the formal technology of chemical engineering became established, centering on a concept that is important for chemical engineers to this day. This concept is called "unit operations." It was devised by a chemical engineer, Arthur D. Little, who started a consulting company that still exists. A unit operation is simply a piece of equipment, such as a tank, distillation column, or heater with a certain amount of raw material or intermediate product passing through it. A chemical engineer analyzes this unit by calculating how much material and energy are in it; what the piece of equipment is doing to change these amounts; and what, if any, chemical reactions are going on inside the equipment.

For example, a common unit operation in mineral processing is calcining. Dustlike particles of a mineral are dropped into a heated chamber, and hot air or a fire is introduced. The process causes the dust to bind together and to be purified of light contaminants, such as water or carbon dioxide. The chemical engineer asks these questions: How much heat do I need to apply to get a certain quantity of calcined material? How complete is the process of driving off contaminants? Is it possible to destroy the chemical products that I want in the final step, and if so, how can I prevent it?

Unit operations came into being as a concept because it enabled chemical engineers to design large-scale, continuous processes to produce larger amounts of product faster and more efficiently. Previously most chemical processes involved dumping something into a vat; heating, mixing, or reacting it; and then opening the vat and shoveling or pouring out the result. Product quality and production costs varied from batch to batch. Unit operation theory also unified processes that appear to be different on the outside, but in reality are the same.

Unit operations also provide a way to conceptualize chemical factories. From the outside, they look simply like a forest of vessels, pipes, smokestacks, and conveyor belts. But from a design engineer's perspective, the factory is simply a long series of unit operations strung together. Pipes or conveyor belts carry the material being processed from one unit to the next. It is successively purified, treated, or reacted and then formed into the desired end product.

The theory of unit operations came along just in time because around 1920 the United States was going through another energy crisis caused by the booming demand for automobiles and gasoline. Petroleum refiners needed to increase capacity and get more gasoline out of each barrel of crude petroleum they received.

Chemicals and Plastics

Chemical engineering got another boost during the late 1930s, and especially during World War II. Again, critical materials were cut off—in this case, natural rubber from the Far East. Around the same time, chemical researchers at Du Pont Company invented nylon. At the time, nylon was looked on as a type of artificial silk. It led to a literal flood of new materials, now know as polymer plastics: polyethylene (the plastic in shopping bags), polycarbonates ("plastic glass"), polyester, acrylics, styrenes, vinyls, phenolics—the list goes on and on.

The commercialization of these polymers helped boost the chemical industry into one of the key parts of the American economy, with annual revenues in the hundreds of billions of dollars. Most of these materials, as well as many chemical liquids or gases in common use today, are derived from crude petroleum. Thus, the oil industry and the chemicals and plastics industries are intertwined (although a far larger volume of petroleum goes to the making of fuel than toward plastics and chemicals).

Energy and the Environment

During the 1950s and 1960s, chemical engineering helped develop nuclear energy, although in later years the field of nuclear engineering came into its own. With knowledge of how petroleum can be processed, chemical engineering crosses over into many aspects of the power utility field. Chemical engineers have also been involved in such areas as solar energy, energy conservation, and coal processing.

Also during the 1950s and 1960s, America began an intensified effort to reconcile the problems of heavy industrial production with the environment. These efforts culminated with the creation of the United States Environmental Protection Agency in 1970. Chemical engineers were in demand then to help devise cleaner production techniques and to clean up past pollution; the demand for such professionals is rising rapidly now.

The demand for chemical engineers reached all-time highs in the late 1970s as the nation prepared for an era of energy independence by developing its own synthetic fuels industry. This industry was to have used such domestic sources of energy as coal or oil shale to reduce the need for imported oil. But the price of oil nose-dived in the early 1980s, the synthetic fuels industry never really got started, and thousands of chemical engineers were out of work.

By the mid-1990s chemical engineering had returned to a more traditional proportion of workers in various industries. Roughly half work in chemical production (or firms that serve this industry) and in energy production. The rest were spread through a diverse array of industries or professional specialties. About 9 percent work for environmental service organizations, according to a survey by the American Institute of Chemical Engineers.

The Current Scene

Most chemical engineers identify their field of work as the chemical process industries (CPI). This category cuts across many types of manufacturing and services. The CPI includes:

- chemicals, including petrochemicals
- fertilizers
- pulp and papermaking
- rubber and plastics
- petroleum refining
- pharmaceuticals
- processed foods
- stone, clay, glass, and ceramics

- energy and fuels
- paints and specialty chemicals
- metals and minerals refining
- engineering design and construction
- environmental services

Most of these industries are traditionally considered "smoke-stack" industries, dealing with taking raw materials from the earth and transforming them into the products we need. For a while in the early 1980s, there was talk of a decline in the smokestack industries in the United States, with production moving abroad and the economy becoming more service oriented. But people soon realized that America couldn't sustain itself without industry; someone has to obtain the essential materials that are the basis of all our finished goods. National wealth is created when something of no value in the ground is transformed to something of high value that people can use.

In a January 2002 report, "The Evolution of Chemical Engineering," several officials of the American Institute of Chemical Engineers examined hiring, research, and business trends that are affecting the chemical engineering profession. In general, they expressed a concern first, that chemical and energy companies had been superseded in pre-eminence by electronics and telecommunications companies in the U.S. economy, and second, that a high proportion of graduating chemical engineers do not work in "traditional" chemistry-oriented industries as their careers progress. But this might be a case of asking whether the glass is half-empty or half-full. Chemical engineers have proven adept at applying their skills in areas such as microelectronics (where, on integrated-circuit production lines, the main skills needed are chemistry and a knowledge of materials) or the evolving industry of biotechnology, whether for pharmaceutical production or for "industrial biotechnology," which is the production of materials and chemicals via biological techniques.

An earlier report from the National Research Council (NRC) successfully anticipated these trends. NRC's report, "Frontiers in Chemical Engineering," was specifically geared toward highlighting research topics that deserved greater attention from engineers, industry, and the federal government. But it can conveniently be looked at as an indicator of where the chemical engineering profession is headed. New research performed today will create jobs for engineers tomorrow. A few chemical engineers are already involved in the newer areas; the more mature ones will see new growth in the future.

The seven areas are as follows:

1. *Biochemical and biomedical engineering.* Because of their understanding of fluids and chemical reactions, chemical engineers have insight into many processes going on in the human body or in forms of life such as animals or bacteria. Today's biotechnology revolution in pharmaceuticals and agriculture, which includes genetic engineering, depends on chemical engineers who extract and purify new drugs.

2. *Electronic, photonic, and recording materials and devices.* This covers the full range of consumer and industrial electronics including microchips, recording tape or compact disks, fiber optics, and printed circuit boards. In addition to being finely designed structures, these objects are physical things that must be manufactured to precise shapes and chemical structures. Microchips, for exam-

ple, are melted silicon that is then crystallized, cut, etched, cleaned, and coated—all chemical processing steps.

3. *Advanced materials.* Yesterday's wonder material, like nylon, is today's commodity. But today's wonder materials are still being developed. These include ceramics that bounce, metals that don't rust, superconductive magnets, and plastics tougher than steel.

4. *Energy and natural resources processing.* The mining and minerals industries, and petroleum production, are quieter today than they were in earlier years, but they have by no means disappeared. New technology is making more gold extraction possible and permitting the recovery of natural gas from uneconomical wells. This field employs a lot of chemical engineers now and could employ many more in the future.

5. *Environmental protection, safety, and hazardous materials.* It is not a coincidence that chemical engineers are experts in dealing with environmental and hazardous material problems, since the CPI manufactures many of these materials. Chemical engineers are being employed by the CPI companies to help minimize waste production. Government agencies, like the Environmental Protection Agency, also hire chemical engineers to regulate polluters.

6. *Computer-assisted process and control engineering.* Modern chemical plants or power utilities are amazingly complex machines, but many of them can be run by a handful of people sitting in a control room. Many chemical plants and power utilities are fully automated. This technology, coming from the computer and electronics industries and adapted to real-world needs, is an especially popular job area today.

7. *Surface and interfacial engineering.* An enormous amount of new technology involves how materials are coated or treated. Many new jobs will be created in this field. For example, it is now possible to extend the life of an artificial hip implant by firing metal atoms into its surface with a machine called an ion implanter. The precise depth and concentration of the atoms can be controlled. Most of the surface engineering work is going on in the electronics industry, metals processing, and production of polymers.

Job Titles

Because chemical engineering covers a broad spectrum of industries, there are many different types of jobs to obtain. Some of the more common ones include the following:

- *Plant engineer.* These engineers are responsible for keeping a chemical process running. They work with machinery operators, monitor product quality, and troubleshoot problems as they occur.

- *Project engineer.* These engineers adapt new technology to existing processes or help build and run new process units. Most chemical process plants are in a continual mode of upgrading or modernizing. Project engineers must know both how a process works and how it could be improved.

- *Design engineer.* When new processes must be created, a design engineer will calculate the sizes and types of equipment appropriate for the process. The pilot plant—a small unit used to calculate full-size designs—is an essential tool for these engineers. Many design engineers work at engineering/construction companies, putting together the building specifications for new plants.

• *Researcher*. Like all engineering disciplines, there are opportunities to perform pure research in chemical processing. Research chemical engineers may work with chemists and physicists, running experiments in a laboratory, or with other chemical engineers in scaling up a process to commercial size.

• *Environmental and workplace-safety engineer*. Chemical engineers can do a lot to prevent pollution and to protect the well-being of plant workers. These engineers help design processes to minimize emissions or reduce waste generation.

• *Control engineer*. One of the dominant trends in chemical engineering today is the adaptation of computers and automatic controls to manufacturing processes. Control engineers help select and install electronic hardware; they also write or oversee the computer software to run the plant.

A Pilot Plant Engineer

Tom is starting the new year with a specific goal in mind: developing the equipment to test a new processing route for purifying water. Pure water is valuable because it can be reused in the production processes of the chemical plant where Tom works. The plant is a huge complex where hundreds of different compounds are manufactured including natural gas, petroleum distillates, and metals. Purified water is also important because if the water can't be reused, it must be discharged to a local river, and strict environmental regulations must be met.

Wastewater from the chemical complex comes to a centralized treatment facility where it is cleaned by an activated-sludge process. Bacteria degrade the organic compounds in the water, creating a thick sludge that can be skimmed from the water. Tom's managers want to reduce the volume of sludge, which is expensive to dispose of, by drying it, i.e., removing more water. Tom is going to try a new process that combines filtration with electricity, which laboratory experiments have shown to be an advantage.

To perform the test, Tom must set up a pilot plant—a small unit, but one big enough to provide engineering numbers through which a full-scale unit can be designed. Pilot plants are critical to new process development; they save the expense of a full-blown unit but provide more details than laboratory test-tube experiments. The equipment cost of Tom's pilot plant will be about $100,000, but a full-size plant will eventually cost about $5 million.

Tom's specific problem on this day is to figure out how to measure the electrochemical values of the sludge mixture. This is tricky because these values are usually measured in a liquid, not in a thick sludge. Tom consults with an instrumentation engineer (who happens to have an electrical engineering degree) and learns of the various types of instruments that can be used. He and his boss also review the flow sheet—a one-page drawing of the essential elements of the process. They determine that the best place to put the instrument will be near the entrance to the vessel where the sludge stream comes in to be filtered and dried. By performing some calculations on the fluid flow near that section of the vessel, they conclude that the sludge will be vigorously mixed, which in turn will mean that the electrochemical instrument will take good readings.

After several months' more work, the test results begin to come in from the pilot plant, and they're good. The addition of an electric field helps to remove 25 percent more water from the sludge. Tom now does a cost analysis, obtaining the price for disposing the sludge on a per-pound basis. With more water removed, the weight of the sludge (relative to the purified water) is lower, reducing disposal costs. On the minus side, however, the cost of electric power and the price of the treatment equipment must be totaled. Overall, the process will reduce water treatment costs by 15 percent, which is sufficient justification for building the plant. Tom writes up a report and now gets ready to deliver it in a presentation to upper management.

Education

Chemical engineering is one of the more intensive engineering programs to study. In addition to learning the basics of engineering, students must also carry six courses in chemistry—almost as much as a full-time chemistry student must attend. These chemistry courses include general chemistry, which nearly all engineering students take; organic chemistry; and physical chemistry.

Specific chemical engineering courses include:

- mass and energy balances
- thermodynamics
- process design
- transport phenomena—the concept of fluids moving through an area and the changes that occur
- chemical engineering economics

In addition, a number of technical electives are usually required. Students seeking to work in biotechnology or pharmaceuticals, for example, might consider taking biology courses. Others may take electives in computer science, materials science, geology, polymer chemistry, or energy.

Mining, Metallurgical, and Petroleum Engineering

No smokestacks are smokier, no earthmovers leave bigger scars, than those used by mining and metallurgical engineers. The mines, refineries, and oil-drilling platforms that these engineers design and manage have a major impact on the environment, and thus environmental sensitivities are ever more important to these professions. By the same token, perhaps no other engineering disciplines are so vital to the manufacturing might of the United States.

It remains truer than ever that the fundamental activity of creating value from natural resources is the path to economic well-being for a country. The majority of American workers are employed in services: running banks, selling consumer goods, providing medical care. These activities represent a trade between a buyer and a seller, and no matter how many times they are repeated, the size of the American economic pie does not increase. However, extracting ore or energy from the ground, turning it into semifinished products, and then completing the transformation either to usable final products, or energy in the form of clean fuels, electricity, or heat does generate wealth. (The other fundamental activities that generate wealth are farming and agriculture.)

The "extractive" industries, as they are sometimes called, have a storied history in the United States. The various gold rushes that helped populate the West; the oil boom, first in a little town called Titusville, Pennsylvania, and then in Texas and other southwestern states; and the coal and ore mines that supplied the muscular steel industry of 1900 helped shaped this country. Most assuredly, mining and oil production continues in the United States today, but in many regards it has receded from the mainstream. Some of the most prolific ore veins and oil reservoirs have emptied out; meanwhile, more productive fields have been found in other parts of the world. Coal production continues at a very high rate within the continental United States, mostly to supply power plants with fuel.

The engineering professions that serve these industries have adapted by becoming more international in scope, with many engineers looking forward to postings in the Middle East, South America, Africa, or Asia during part of their careers. Engineering research has developed new techniques to win metal from poorer ores, or to extract more petroleum or gas from old fields. Offshore oil and gas exploration and production have been successfully applied in the Gulf of Mexico, and thence to harsh environments around the world.

Another change that has affected these professions is that the engineers working to purify natural resources—oil, metal, and minerals—have evolved toward materials science and engineering (this will be treated in the next chapter). Developing refining methods for high-tech metals, or for ceramics that will be used in microelectronics, is now its own specialty. There is some crossover between the two, to be sure, but today's engineering student has a pretty clear-cut choice between working to get minerals and energy from the ground, or developing processes and products from those materials in laboratories and factories.

A relatively small number of engineers now study in the disciplines of mining or geological engineering and petroleum engineering. The graduating class of 2000 had 623 B.S.E. graduates;

this is up from only 417 in 1991, according to data from the Engineering Workforce Commission. According to the Bureau of Labor Statistics, there are 15,500 mining or petroleum engineers working currently, and the outlook is for that number to decline, by 4.5 percent, by 2010. On the brighter side, starting salaries tend to be on the high side, especially for petroleum engineers, who get offers of $53,000 according to various sources.

History

The history of mining and metallurgical engineering is one of the factors that helps define human civilization; archaeologists date the transition from the Stone Age to the Bronze Age to the Iron Age starting about five thousand years ago.

Mining and metal refining developed gradually over the centuries, spurred by the discoveries of new metals, the desire for precious metals (gold and silver), and the needs of developing technologies. In the New World the availability of gold and silver in South America was one of the driving forces for Spanish conquest. In North America, although there were many searches for precious metals, little happened in this regard until the mid-1800s, when gold was discovered in California and the West. Coal mining, on the other hand, was a major industry throughout that century. Huge iron ore deposits in Minnesota (the Mesabi Range, which is still being mined) helped get the newly established steel industry off and running in the late 1800s. Henry Bessemer, an English scientist, is generally credited with inventing the Bessemer process for producing low-carbon iron that could readily be converted to steel.

Production methods for other metals and minerals were being developed rapidly in the late 1800s, including techniques for producing aluminum, copper, zinc, and lead; and glass, gypsum plaster, and cement for concrete.

These events helped establish the professional status of engineers specializing in metals and minerals. The American Institute of Mining, Metallurgical and Petroleum Engineers (AIME) was founded in 1871; an Iron and Steel Division, highlighting the increased importance of steelmaking, was established in 1912; a Petroleum Division in 1922; and a Coal Division in 1930. In later years the organization decided to decentralize, and the various divisions became autonomous groups under the AIME umbrella. Today these groups are known as the Society of Petroleum Engineers, the Society of Mining Engineers, and the Metallurgy and Iron and Steel societies, which later became the Minerals, Metals and Materials Society, known by its acronym, TMS.

As the American West began to be explored in earnest in the latter half of the 1800s, many new sources of metal were found, including copper in Arizona and Idaho, lead and zinc in Colorado, and aluminum in Washington and Oregon. But these sources were limited in size and purity, and the search went around the world. By the mid-1900s, important sources of ore for American industry were in South America, Africa, Canada, and the Far East.

The first well drilled to produce crude oil was in Titusville, Pennsylvania, in 1859. It was all of seventy feet deep. By comparison, wells are being drilled today through a half-mile of water (in the Gulf of Mexico), digging into the ground for more than another five miles. Getting from the earliest well technology to the latest has been the work of the petroleum engineering profession. By and large it divides into two functions: exploring for oil and then producing it. Production can be simply drilling a hole and attaching a pump (or a throttling valve if the pressure of the field is so high that oil would gush forth). Alternatively, petroleum engineers are learning how to use detergent chemicals and solvents to "scrub" oil out of what had been considered an exhausted well.

Like the mining industry, much of today's oil production occurs away from the continental United States, which has been surveyed and drilled extensively over the past century. The Prudhoe Bay oil field on the North Slope of Alaska was the last major oil find in the United States. Production of oil has dropped from just over ten million barrels a year in its peak years of the early 1980s to around six million today. On the other hand, the importance of gas production has risen, as this has become the fuel of choice for environmental reasons. Gas production has gone from about sixteen trillion cubic feet per year in the early 1990s to about nineteen trillion today.

Exploration, Extraction, and Production

The major American oil firms remain dominant forces in the world market for exploration and production. This is good news for engineering students, who have the opportunity to work abroad through one of these firms.

Exploring for, and producing, oil calls on a host of technologies. Exploration engineers will use seismographic techniques, satellite photographs, and underground rock samples to locate an oil pocket. A major development in this step has been the use of the latest supercomputers to process huge amounts of data on underground formations in order to locate reservoirs more easily. Not so long ago, an oil exploration company considered itself a successful operator if one out of six wells was a commercial producer—a very high-stakes gamble, given the cost of drilling a well. Today's technology has enabled oil companies to drop that to almost one out of two, which are certainly better odds.

Once a site has been selected, a drilling crew sets up a rig. The petroleum engineer monitors the types of rocks and soil the drill cuts through and can further test the site by running a "string" of electronic instruments down the well to analyze geological conditions. There is an interesting combination of outdoors work—sometimes taking place in the most remote regions of the world—and high-technology tasks in computer-equipped offices. Another important trend in drilling is known as multidirectional drilling. Drillers are now able to dig to a certain depth, then fan out in a variety of directions to seek the best oil-bearing formations. Some wells have many branches, at different levels, to obtain as much petroleum or gas as possible from a formation.

Domestic ore extraction and processing have been a declining industry in recent years, caused primarily by the exhaustion of easily extracted ores in the United States and the discovery of new resources in other parts of the world. There are notable exceptions: the ability of researchers to develop new extraction methods allows mining companies to successfully exploit low-grade ores. But one of the main accommodations that mining companies, and the engineering-consulting firms that advise them, have made is to internationalize their business, so that they are either operating mines outright in other parts of the world, or providing consulting services to overseas mining companies.

Technologically, one of the most notable achievements in coal mining has been the development of what is called "longwall" extraction. This involves literally building a robotic machine in place, inside a mine, to carve into a vein of coal along a wide path, rather than having individual miners operating powered cutting tools. The technology has greatly increased the productivity of mining labor. Another very specialized part of mining technology is used for civil engineering projects, such as tunnels crossing mountain ranges or rivers. During the 1990s a historic threshold was passed when the "Chunnel"—the English Channel tunnel—was completed. Similar projects are performed for water transportation systems.

Education

Education for petroleum engineering combines several aspects of civil engineering, chemical engineering, and geology. Students take courses in geology, hydrogeology, and chemistry to understand the dynamics of underground wells. There are more courses on reservoir engineering—the practices of maintaining a field's capacity once extraction begins.

In mining or geological engineering, the educational emphasis is on geology and the techniques for building stable underground structures. Mine safety is a very significant specialty within the field. A modern underground mine is vastly more complex today than in past decades; it wasn't so long ago that mining was among the most dangerous of any occupations, and seldom a year went by when there wasn't a major mine collapse or fire that could kill hundreds. Today these disasters are but a dim memory, at least in the United States.

Job Titles

The structure of job classifications varies widely from industry to industry in mining and petroleum engineering. Here are some of the more prominent job titles:

• *Exploration geophysicist.* The search for oil or gas reservoirs involves highly advanced computational technology and knowledge of geology. Oil companies have been among the leaders in seeking the most powerful supercomputers to perform these analyses. The technology now allows the specialists to look at visual representations of underground formations and get a sense of how a formation is situated.

• *Oil platform engineer.* An offshore platform shares as many characteristics with an oceangoing vessel as it does with an oil well. (In fact, many of them now float on the ocean, tied to a well with cables rather than the older "jack-up" technology of building a stationary tower that reaches the ocean bottom.) These engineers might be involved in designing or constructing the platform, either on land or in place on the sea. They can also be involved with running the platform, making sure that the heavy machinery that powers the drilling equipment is functioning suitably.

• *Reservoir engineer.* Once a well is in place, its operation is more of running the machinery than of engineering. However, it is only a limited period of time, depending on the nature of the formation, before techniques must be used to pressurize the field to draw more petroleum or gas from it. Steam or water can be injected to serve this purpose. Now the reservoir engineer must analyze well data to figure out how best to coax the resource from the ground. New wells might be dug, or the well might be redirected with multidirectional drilling.

• *Plant superintendent.* Mines and metal smelters are geared specifically toward producing the desired metal or mineral. The key technical person is the superintendent, who oversees production, labor, and costs. There is constant pressure to keep the mills running as various types of ores are brought in or as the mine's topography changes in following a rich vein of ore.

• *Environmental manager.* Because mining, metals, and materials production have a high potential for pollution, extra efforts are expended on environmental control. These include treatment of exhaust gases from smokestacks, water treatment of process water, and disposal of wastes or residues.

4

Modern Engineering

This chapter is so titled not because the disciplines in other chapters are old-fashioned, but simply because all of the professions discussed in this chapter evolved in the twentieth century. The largest of the disciplines in this chapter, industrial/manufacturing engineering, originated in the growing complexity of production technology. A key milestone was the development of the assembly line at Ford Motor Company, where new techniques allowed a complete car to flow out of the factory every couple of minutes. For the time, the development was revolutionary.

A similar story could be told of other engineering disciplines. Aerospace/aeronautical engineering arose from the new technology of heavier-than-air flight. Materials science/engineering arose as the ability to tailor refined or synthetic materials (metals, ceramics, and polymers) became understood by manufacturers. Petroleum engineering stepped into the spotlight as the needs of the internal combustion engine (especially in automobiles) ballooned in the first couple of decades of the century. The computer became a reality shortly after World War II and has since become a dominant force in our society. Finally the growing concentration of manufacturers, cities, and homes has created the need for environmental engineering—adapting technology to preventing pollution of the air, water, and land.

Industrial/Manufacturing Engineering

One of the most important words to manufacturers is productivity—the ratio between hours of work expended and the volume of products made or work performed. What is the best way to arrange the elements of a manufacturing process to achieve the highest productivity? That is the question industrial and manufacturing engineers address on a daily basis.

There is a strong overlap between two types of engineers involved with manufacturing productivity. The industrial engineer is a graduate of a four-year program with the same academic background as the other engineers listed in the previous chapter. Most manufacturing engineers, on the other hand, are graduates of programs in engineering technology. There are some industrial engineers called manufacturing engineers; conversely, it is possible to get a degree in industrial engineering technology. The big difference between the two is the type of undergraduate education that engineers and engineering technologists receive. Engineering technology is more applied learning with courses targeted toward specific activities or industries. Industrial engineers receive a broader, more theoretically oriented education. Thus, while both can and do work for manufacturers, most technologists are restricted to that field of employment. Industrial engineers can find work at hospitals, construction firms, transportation services, and business consulting firms. This section will focus on all industrial engineers, as well as the number of engineering technologists who focus on manufacturing.

Combined, these engineers and technologists number roughly 198,000, according to the Bureau of Labor Statistics. It projects that the field will grow by 6 percent—slightly below the average for all professions—by the year 2010.

History

Industrial engineering traces its roots back to the new complexities of manufacturing on assembly lines, which were first organized for the production of automobiles and agricultural harvesters and then extended to textiles, food processing, and the assembly of fabricated parts of all types. In the 1910s and 1920s, the field became formalized as "scientific management," in the belief that some fundamentally new ways of managing workers had been created that had a stronger mathematical base than the seat-of-the-pants management styles of the past. Frederick Taylor was the leading developer of this philosophy.

Manufacturing complexity continued to increase, but the Great Depression interfered with any major technological progress. Machine tool engineers and machinists in the Detroit area gathered in 1932 to see what could be done. They decided to organize what was then called the American Society of Tool Engineers, which evolved in 1960 into the American Society of Tool and Manufacturing Engineers. The name was again changed in 1970 to the Society of Manufacturing Engineers (SME).

During World War II, the need for enormous amounts of war materials sent a jolt through industry. Out of this heightened interest in improving manufacturing productivity, the Institute of Industrial Engineering was formed in 1948. Industrial growth and productivity boomed during the 1950s and 1960s, but hit some snags in the 1970s. By the end of that decade, the woeful state of manufacturing in the United States relative to other countries in the world became apparent as imports flooded the steel, automobile, consumer electronics, and other industries. Since then, American industry has been on a productivity and quality-improvement kick. This drive has opened up many new opportunities for industrial and manufacturing engineers. Between 1977 and 1987, the membership of SME nearly doubled, to about eighty thousand.

Industrial Specialties

The quality and productivity battles that American industry is waging against the rest of the world's manufacturers are still going strong. Nearly all manufacturers are looking closely at their production lines and workforces. A technological background is important for nearly all types of manufacturing managers.

The Institute of Industrial Engineers is organized into three societies (the Society for Health Systems; for Engineering and Management Systems; and the Aerospace and Defense Society), nine interest groups, and eight divisions:

Interest Groups
Computer and information systems
Consultants
Electronics industry
Engineering design
Government

Process industries
Production and inventory control
Retail
Logistics, transportation, and distribution

Divisions
Energy, environment, and plant engineering
Engineering economy
Facilities planning and design
Financial services
Operations research
Quality control and reliability
Utilities
Ergonomics and work measurement

The latter division, in a way, represents the classical scientific management that is the heart of industrial engineering. In order to maximize productivity, industrial engineers will stand by workers on an assembly line with a stopwatch and record the motions workers make as they complete tasks. This time and motion study is then translated into the procedures that all workers are to follow. Most recently American firms have adopted the model of European factories. One or several workers are responsible for all the assembly steps of a unit or component, rather than simply screwing one part onto another and passing the result down the line.

The Society of Manufacturing Engineers divides its membership into fifteen technical activity areas, based on the specific manufacturing technology involved. These include material forming, finishing, robotics, sensors, automated fastening, composites, and manufacturing management.

Job titles range from production manager to quality assurance engineer to control engineer. Because both industrial and manufacturing engineers are so intimately involved with workers and plant management, this background can be a sturdy steppingstone into corporate management.

Industrial engineers study the normal load of fundamental engineering courses and then select from a variety of specialties such as labor relations, industrial psychology, computers, economics, and business management.

Aerospace/Aeronautical Engineering

To fly! That ancient dream became a reality at Kitty Hawk, North Carolina, in the dawning days of the twentieth century. Now, almost a century later, flying can be done in a bewildering array of balloons, satellites, rockets, airplanes, helicopters, jetliners, and gliders.

The technical people responsible for keeping all these devices aloft, and those who design and build new types, are aerospace/aeronautical engineers. (In this book the term "aerospace" covers both of these terms.) Aerospace engineers aren't the only ones who work on aircraft; mechanical, electrical, computer, and materials engineers are also well represented. However, aerospace engineers have the central responsibility of designing the shape and performance characteristics of the craft and of specifying a propulsion system and guidance controls.

There are about fifty thousand aerospace engineers at work today, according to federal data; the number is projected to rise by 14 percent by the year 2010, an average growth rate. Aerospace engineers who have recently graduated get salary offers of around $48,000, according to various surveys.

History

The federal government has been a prime mover of aerospace technology throughout the twentieth century. After the inaugural flight of the Wright brothers, the government began producing planes for the army, which wanted to use them for battlefield surveillance. The United States Post Office also became involved, seeing airplanes as an obvious delivery vehicle for the mail. Around this time, William Goddard, a scientist, was working in near-total obscurity on rocket technology—a field that the Defense Department practically ignored until after World War II.

Enough of an airplane industry had developed by the early 1930s to warrant the establishment of two professional societies—the American Rocket Society (1930) and the Institute of Aerospace Sciences (1932); these societies merged in 1963 to form the American Institute of Aeronautics and Astronautics, Inc. (AIAA). Today the Institute has about thirty-one thousand members.

Aircraft design and construction took a huge jump during World War II as all sorts of fighter aircraft, bombers, and cargo planes were developed. After the war some of these designs were adopted to civilian uses, such as the venerable Douglas DC-3. The development of the turbojet created a new class of aircraft and opened a new era of international travel. The term "jet set" was coined in the early 1960s as a reference to the possibilities of world travel. Commercial aviation (i.e., nonmilitary aviation) is now a business of more than $100 billion annually, and the construction of commercial aircraft and equipment is tens of billions more.

In the 1960s the American space program hit its stride with the objective of landing a man on the moon before the end of the decade. This happened in 1969, and it was followed by a handful of later flights. Spacelab was built (later to fall to earth), and then the major portion of funding from the National Aeronautics and Space Administration (NASA) was shifted to the Space Shuttle, which is in use today.

Also after World War II, the rocket became a critical component in the nuclear defense arsenal of the United States. Rockets were also the main method of lofting satellites into space, especially communications satellites that permitted live, around-the-world transmissions.

The end of the Cold War between the United States and the former Soviet Union has had a dramatic impact on the aerospace engineering profession. Through most of the 1990s the United States was "building down" (a euphemism for reducing) the size of its military forces, cutting back on the production of aircraft, and stretching out the development cycle for new-generation aircraft. The tragic events of September 11, 2001, did many things, including signaling an end to the post–Cold War era and the beginning of a new era where military force again becomes a priority. The first federal budgets in the aftermath of September 11 called for a major increase in military and security spending. At the same time, the military action in Afghanistan and other parts of the world will require replenishment of military hardware.

Throughout the post–WW II era, defense spending dictated much of the growth of the aerospace industry. Now such activities as space-borne telecommunications, commercial aviation, and air cargo represent alternative career paths. Although it can be expected that the military buildup to take place in the next several years will dramatically raise employment prospects for aerospace engineers, at some point a new balance will be achieved between employment dedicated to military projects and nonmilitary businesses.

Specializations

Aerospace engineers have learned a tremendous amount about the performance of materials and structures under extreme stress. This knowledge is required for developing new aircraft, and it can also be adapted to other fields such as land-based transportation, power generators, electronic controls, and related areas. Thus, though most aerospace engineers work for large government contractors, their expertise can be applied in many other areas.

AIAA identifies seven areas of concentration among its members. They are as follows:

1. *Propulsion*. This is the means by which aircraft move onward and upward.
2. *Fluid mechanics*. The fluid in this case is air, flowing into jet engines or over wings.
3. *Thermodynamics*. This deals with handling extremes of heat and cold in an aircraft—even in the cold vacuum of space.
4. *Structures*. Aircraft must be able to withstand the intense stresses of takeoff, flight, and landing.
5. *Celestial mechanics*. How does one predict that a satellite launched this year will pass close by Saturn three or five years from now? Celestial mechanics provides the answers.
6. *Acoustics*. Acoustics—the study of sound—is important to prevent vibration and noise pollution from aircraft.

7. *Guidance and control.* This is another obvious element of aircraft design. Some of today's aircraft are so complex that a pilot cannot fly the plane alone; an onboard computer helps by making rapid adjustments.

Training for aerospace engineering includes the standard courses all engineering students take, plus a list of specialized courses including aerodynamic design, advanced mathematics, fluid mechanics, electronics, propulsion systems, trajectory dynamics, and structural analysis. Nearly one out of three aerospace engineers goes on to get a master's degree.

Materials Engineering

In the description of mining and minerals engineering in the previous chapter, we saw how the technology to extract and refine ore from the ground set the stage for additional technological development to improve materials important in manufacturing and construction. This evolution accelerated during the twentieth century, most notably in the development of plastic polymers and other synthetic materials. By the middle of the century, a "materials revolution" was well under way, with a host of new materials entering the marketplace. Almost invariably, the word "miracle" would be attached to these materials—metals that did not rust, fibers that were stronger than the plant fibers that they replaced in clothing, ceramics that made microelectronics possible. Although the nuclear research of the era was aimed at far different goals, it is interesting to note that the medieval fantasy of transmuting lead into gold became technically possible during these years.

The engineering professions were at the forefront of this effort, taking new discoveries out of laboratories and turning them into tonnage quantities of consumer goods. The Metals, Minerals and Materials Society (TMS) was organized out of parts of the American Institute of Mining, Metals and Petroleum Engineering during the 1930s. A decade earlier, metals processors in the Midwest had joined together to form what would eventually be called the American Society for Metals (later, ASM International). The automotive and aircraft industries created a need for newer, higher-strength metals. The use of electricity to refine metals grew in importance. Finally, beginning in the 1950s but growing in intensity with each passing year, the needs of the microelectronics industry for ultrapure silicon, exotic new minerals such as gallium arsenide, or rare earth minerals such as tellurium or yttrium, spurred new technology for minerals processing.

Ceramic engineering has been on a somewhat different course. Most semiconductors used in microelectronics are, in fact, a type of ceramic, and there has been considerable information-sharing between ceramic engineering and electronics engineering. The fiber-optics industry, which has grown from practically nothing a decade ago to a major component of telecommunications and networking systems, also involve ceramic engineering. (One of the leading companies in this field, Corning, has mostly divested its well-known glassware and ceramic businesses to concentrate on fiber optics.)

Most ceramics are used in construction—cement and concrete, wallboard, and glass windows. New technology has affected sections of the industry from time to time, but imports are not as much of a problem. Rather, the ups and downs of the construction business affect industrial growth. For most of the 1980s, this growth was strong, but lately it has begun to settle down.

Both ceramics and metals are affected by the other major material—polymers. Materials engineers and chemical engineers share this technological territory. Many of the major producers of polymer raw materials are also the producers of finished goods such as textiles or composite structures.

The last century also witnessed the explosion in polymer and plastics, derived mostly from petroleum or gas feedstocks. As polymers increase in strength and durability, they offer a lower-cost substitute for glass and metal. More and more bottles for foods and beverages are now being fabricated from plastic. The automotive industry is increasing the plastic content of cars and reducing the metal content. All-plastic airplanes are on the drawing board. The dramatic Stealth bomber that was unveiled in 1988 by Northrop Corporation features wings and a fuselage made from high-tech composites that combine glass fibers with plastic resins. The use of plastic makes the aircraft lighter and less visible to radar sensing. The Society of Plastics Engineers, Inc., was formed in 1942. A year later, the Society for the Advancement of Material and Process Engineering (SAMPE) was formed, mostly for bringing together technologists working in the aerospace industry.

The Bureau of Labor Statistics counts 33,000 materials engineers working currently, and expects growth in the occupation to be average through 2010, reaching 34,800 by then. Starting salaries are around $50,000.

The Current Scene

The materials industries jumped in prominence a couple of years ago with the discovery of "warm" superconductors. These are a combination of copper and rare earth minerals that can conduct electricity with no power loss. Previous superconductors needed to be kept at nearly absolute zero temperature—a freezing −460° F. It may be possible to develop superconductors that can carry current at room temperature, thus reducing the cost of conveying it.

Materials engineers, particularly those working in aerospace, have become adept at combining the toughness of glass or ceramics with the fracture resistance of plastics or other polymers. The result is known technically as a composite material, and it shows up in the fiberglass hulls of pleasure craft, automobile body panels, and construction materials. Even forestry companies have gotten into the act, combining layers of wood with plastics or polymeric glues to create strong, yet inexpensive plywood. All of these are products of materials science and engineering.

These advances, occurring in high-tech aerospace or microelectronics manufacturing overshadow more traditional materials, but there is plenty of activity on those fronts. In the steel industry, for example, it is now common to build minimills that don't process raw iron, but use scrap steel instead. As the name implies, this practice dramatically reduces the size of a mill.

That minimills succeed in using scrap steel is a message to other materials producers; recycling and reuse are in. The growing shortage of disposal space for garbage and waste means that more materials recycling must be established. Aluminum, glass, copper, lead, and steel producers are already good recyclers. Now plastics and paper manufacturers are cranking up capacity and technology for recycling these materials.

Perhaps the most exciting aspect of materials science and engineering today is the replacement of body parts with synthetic materials. "Biocompatible" metals, ceramics, and plastics are now improving the lives of people who have lost limbs, whose joints have degraded, or who need artificial blood, skin, or organs because of injury or disease. Such biomaterials must pass a rigorous series of testing and evaluation, and the medical professions are at least as involved as the engineering profession (a powerful combination of degrees in this regard is to get an undergraduate degree in materials engineering and combine it with an M.D. degree).

Here are some of the common job titles in materials science and engineering:

• *Production engineer.* Most materials manufacturing organizations have large factories with expensive machinery; many of these production lines run twenty-four hours a day. A production line can range from a microelectronics fabrication ("fab") line to the rolling mills of a steel mill. Production engineers generally work the daylight shift and are responsible for monitoring the productivity and quality of the manufacturing lines. When new equipment is installed (as it always is), the new production procedures must be worked out.

• *Process engineer.* A process engineer is also concerned with production, but more from a design standpoint. Complex manufacturing steps must be coordinated, and there are technical measures of the flow through the production line or where production reaches bottlenecks.

• *QA/QC manager.* "QA/QC" stands for "quality assurance/quality control" (there is a technical difference between the two). Most manufacturing processes run at a high pace, so the sooner an out-of-specification product can be identified, the more quickly the production line can be adjusted. Many materials engineers spend time in laboratories, running tests and performing evaluations as part of this effort. The best manufacturers of a particular material, regardless of its composition, want to be able to adjust its characteristics to meet customers' requirements, and this effort requires constant tinkering with the ingredients and processes of manufacturing.

- *Design engineer.* When a new material is proposed for a certain application, or when new applications evolve, design engineers will study the problem, propose appropriate materials, then build and test prototypes. The effort in the automotive industry to develop lighter but stronger components is a good example of this.

Melt Shop Manager

The heart of a steel mill is the melt shop—the location where a furnace liquefies metal in a searingly hot vessel. The chemical composition of the "melt," as it is called, is then checked and adjusted, and the molten metal is poured out to form ingots. The ingots are then flattened, smoothed, or cut into standard shapes.

But Tom is the proud engineer responsible for developing a relatively new method of making steel called thin-slab continuous casting. A thin slab is about an inch thick. It is now possible, and conventional, to cast slabs that are six or eight inches thick in a continuous caster. From there the slab is rolled to thinner dimensions in a section of the plant called a "hot strip." Finally it is cold-rolled to form sheet steel. Thousands of tons of coiled sheet steel are sold annually to auto and appliance makers to produce their products. If Tom's project succeeds, it will eliminate most of the hot strip, which would dramatically reduce the cost of producing sheet steel. The big problem, though, is to produce steel with few flaws or impurities because this high-quality steel is being used on the outer surfaces of products. No one would buy a new car with holes or pieces of slag on the fenders.

Tom is not alone in this effort; the entire company management is watching its progress daily. Today Tom's challenge is to improve the heat retention of the molten steel as it comes out of the furnace. If it cools too quickly, cracks form as it is being drawn into the thin slab. To research the problem, Tom has set a couple of dozen thermocouples (high-temperature thermometers) in the channel where the molten steel flows. As it goes by, he gets a set of readings of the temperature in each section of the channel.

Tom finds that the middle of the channel is hot enough, but that the sides are too cool, sometimes even causing solidified steel to stick to them. There are two choices readily available: adding heat to the sides of the channel, or insulating it better so that it doesn't cool as rapidly. Both have their pros and cons, but Tom senses that insulation may be the more dependable, and less expensive, route to go. He now begins researching the variety of insulating bricks that are available. He will get a sample of each material from their manufacturers and then run tests on all of them.

Education

The most common designation in academic departments for the materials field is materials science and engineering. Many universities have standing departments of metallurgical, ceramics, or polymer engineering as well. Materials "science" tends to refer more to the analysis of materials and development of new ones, while materials "engineering" tends to refer to manufacturing or working with materials for specific purposes, but this distinction is a small one. The curricula of all these programs have a generous helping of chemistry, combined with chemistry-heavy courses in metallurgy, ceramics, polymers, and others.

Not all engineering departments try, or want, to cram all the necessary study into a four-year undergraduate program. Five-year programs leading to a professional or master's-level degree are common. Two academic tracks have developed for many materials engineers: a bachelor's degree that can lead to a job in production and a master's or Ph.D. degree for design, research, and development. Courses for these programs include:

- organic chemistry
- metallurgy
- strength of materials
- polymer science
- thermodynamics
- mechanical design
- microelectronics fabrication

Environmental Engineering

When most people think about doing something good for the environment, they usually think about saving wildlife or preserving forests; maybe they also think about recycling materials or buying a fuel-efficient car. But there is a profession whose primary objective is preserving and even improving the environment around us: environmental engineering.

The roots of this profession, at least in the United States, lie in the efforts of municipalities across the country to develop adequate water resources. This, in turn, has two aspects: water treatment, to make water potable, if it isn't naturally; and wastewater treatment, to process the waste streams so that they can safely be discharged to rivers or coasts. This field was called sanitary engineering until the late 1960s, when, with the popular effort to address environmental damage that culminated in the first Earth Day (1970), environmentalism "arrived." On a somewhat parallel path, many cities needed to address air pollution problems in the early 1900s; this effort resulted in a profession, that of air quality inspector, and a professional society, the Air Pollution Control Association (now known as the Air and Waste Management Association). Both these professional affiliations found their natural governmental aspect when the Environmental Protection Agency was formed in that same year.

In the 1980s environmental engineering was one of the hottest careers going. Environmental protection didn't just "happen" in that decade; it was built on concerns and technologies that had been maturing for many decades. But the momentum to stop damaging the environment and to repair previous injuries took on new intensity at that time, and new regulations spurred the growth of hundreds of companies. Since then, environmentalism has slowed considerably, but it remains at a much higher level than it was ten years ago.

Most engineers who work in the environmental field start by obtaining a civil engineering degree. This is fine, but many observers of the environmental field believe that a different curriculum should be taught. Specifically, they believe civil engineering should be combined with knowledge of biology: microbes; ecological systems, such as forests or estuaries; and biochemistry. There are a limited number of schools where environmental engineering is taught under that specific title. More often, one takes an environmental concentration in civil, chemical, or mechanical engineering.

The American Academy of Environmental Engineers, with about twenty-five hundred members, represents the certified, experienced environmental professionals. Several thousand civil engineers within the American Society of Civil Engineers specialize in environmental issues; a similar case exists within the American Institute of Chemical Engineers. The U.S. Bureau of Labor Statistics's count of environmental engineers is fifty-two thousand, and it projects a faster-than-average growth rate of 26 percent for the profession. A total of 697 students obtained a B.S. degree in environmental engineering in 2000, according to the Engineering Workforce Commission; in the same year, 723 obtained their master's degree.

Except where there is an obvious hazard, such as a smog alert or an outbreak of a waterborne disease, most environmental problems develop over a long period of time and can take a long time to correct. For this reason (and others), much of the effort that American society dedicates to the environment happens due to regulation. From its earliest days to the present, environmental protection is a political and social issue, as much as it is a technological one. The current debate over global warming, for example, echoes earlier debates over water and land use, hazardous waste disposal, deforestation, and wilderness preservation. "Government regulations will largely determine the number of available [job] openings," is how the Bureau of Labor Statistics sums up the career prospects of the field.

Job Opportunities

Today's environmental engineers work for local, state, and federal government and for engineering firms that perform consulting work for government agencies. Environmental engineers also work in industries, such as organic chemicals or metals extraction, that have the potential to create significant amounts of pollution. A study by Rutgers University in 1994 found that half of the environmental professionals working in industry were in chemicals, petroleum and coal, or primary metals. Although some engineers in industry are able to specialize in the control of air pollution, water pollution, or solid waste, at many companies these responsibilities are merged into an environmental services department.

The American Academy of Environmental Engineers recognizes seven areas of specialization for which it gives certificates:

- Air pollution control
- General environmental engineering
- Hazardous waste management
- Industrial hygiene engineering
- Radiation protection engineering
- Solid waste management
- Water supply/wastewater engineering

Job titles range widely, as does the type of employer. Moreover, the field is evolving rapidly, generating new types of jobs. Some of the more common ones in existence today are:

- *Site manager.* The site manager works on EPA-sponsored hazardous-waste cleanup projects.

- *Compliance officer.* This officer works on the environmental-control systems at a manufacturing plant.

• *Design engineer.* The responsibility for this position in an engineering construction firm involves developing environmental systems for private or public works.

• *Enforcement official.* The enforcement official works for a state environmental agency or for the United States Environmental Protection Agency.

The career path for many environmental engineers begins at state or federal environmental agencies, which provide training in technology and regulatory issues. With this background many engineers then move on to higher-paying jobs in private industry.

Computer Engineering

The booming computer industry has two basic types of technical experts: engineers for computer hardware, and computer scientists and programmers for computer software. Midway between the two is the computer engineer, who must be aware of trends at both ends of the spectrum.

Computer engineering is a relatively new field, having developed as an academic program over the past twenty or so years. Many students studying electrical engineering and specializing in microelectronics call themselves computer engineers, but the electrical engineering curriculum tends to emphasize hardware over software. Conversely, it is possible to study computer science in college and graduate with an understanding of both hardware and software by taking microelectronics courses. Because of this overlap, many schools have begun offering degrees in computer engineering. The computer engineering curriculum offers more software courses than the normal electrical engineering major and more hardware courses than the average computer science major. Computer engineering is targeted more specifically at the computer industry.

The field has also been affected greatly by new technology. In its early years, the number of computer configurations was fairly stable. There were large, fast mainframe computers for running many different operations rapidly, over large sets of data, for an entire corporation. There were minicomputers, which were smaller, slower, but less expensive and suitable for fulfilling the computer needs of a department. And the microcomputer, better known as the personal computer (PC), was being offered for the single user. Everything having to do with computing underwent a transformation in the mid-1990s as the implications of the Internet were realized. Now, people talk about "application service providers"— a technology whereby a computer might be in one place, and the software that it is running is in another (and the end user in a third location, anywhere in the world!).

Since then, the supercomputer has evolved into a very fast number-crunching machine for scientific applications. The PC has become a major force in the computer world; around fifty million units are shipped each year in the United States. Meanwhile, specialized computers have appeared for artificial intelligence programming, enhanced graphics processing, and high-speed factory automation equipment. And the general structure of these computers ranges from single-processor (one central "brain" that performs computations) to multiprocessor designs. Some of the latter are set up for a form of computing called "parallel processing," which allows the computer to execute programs more rapidly.

Even more general than the type of box in which micro-processors are housed are computing applications that have only a vague relationship to a "computer." A good example of this is the digital switching equipment that telecommunications companies use to route phone calls. A similar device specifically for the Internet is the router, which has become a multibillion-dollar business in less than a decade. At the other end of the computing scale, there are personal digital assistants, MP3 audio players, game consoles—even the latest cell phones feature an impressive array of computing functions. A computing engineering student could intend, for example, to develop a new and better game box, but soon wind up creating visualization software for oil companies to analyze underground geology. The computing platform (hardware) can match up in odd and unexpected ways with the application (software).

Job Opportunities

All these styles, or "architectures," for computers have created a boom for people trained in computer design—computer engineers. The computer field is huge and dynamic. Jobs—even companies—are not stable. But it remains one of the most entrepreneurial fields of technology, one where careers can move upward rapidly. But it is also possible to have one's employer go out of business overnight.

Most computer engineers work at firms that design and build computers. Some also find opportunities in the much larger realm of computer users. Banks, insurance companies, universities, and research groups all have a need for engineers who thoroughly understand computer hardware, yet are also aware of how computers are being put to use. Computer engineers in the latter position help their employers set up suitable computer departments and help specify the networks, communication equipment, and printers for outputting data.

Job demand is very strong for the computer engineer. Students have been flocking to computer engineering programs. In the late 1970s there were a thousand or so B.S. graduates; in 2000 there were just under ten thousand B.S.E. graduates and just over five thousand earning an M.S.E. degree. According to the Bureau of Labor Statistics, there were 60,000 computer hardware engineers working in 2000, and the field will grow faster than average, reaching 75,000 professionals in 2010. Starting salaries are around $52,000, according to academic sources. And, to recap the comments in the section on electrical/electronics engineering, the Bureau of Labor Statistics identifies a profession of "computer software engineers" that includes people with backgrounds in either computer engineering or in computer science. That field is enumerated as having 697,000 practitioners currently and shows a tremendous growth projection—95 percent—to about 1.4 million by 2010. There will be numerous computer engineers within that field.

5

Engineering Specialties

THE MANY ENGINEERING disciplines listed so far by no means exhaust the various fields of study available. Whatever your interest, there is probably an engineering department devoted to that study, or to something that comes awfully close. Many schools also have an independent-study option that would allow you to exercise your curiosities.

The list of possible fields of study is greatly expanded at the master's degree level. So much has to be crammed into an undergraduate education that it is hard to develop both a broad, general knowledge of engineering and sufficient understanding of some specialized fields. You may think that going to graduate school would require too much time or money. Only about a quarter of all undergraduate engineering students go to graduate school. However, many of those students are earning their master's degrees while already starting their working careers. They do so by attending graduate school at night. This gives students an income while they are still getting trained. Many companies also cover the cost of tuition for graduate school.

The following are some of the more well-known engineering specialties:

- biomedical/bioengineering
- agricultural engineering
- nuclear engineering
- marine/ocean engineering and naval architecture
- safety and fire protection engineering
- optical engineering
- automotive engineering
- textile engineering
- energy engineering
- heating, ventilating, air-conditioning, and refrigeration engineering
- systems engineering/operations research
- engineering history/technical writing

Biomedical/Bioengineering

Biomedical engineering or bioengineering is developing into two types of specialties: the engineering design of body parts, especially human ones, and the application of the biotechnology revolution.

During the 1950s and 1960s, the growing body of knowledge about how engineering systems worked—structures, fluid flow, chemical reactions, electronics—led to a belief that the human body could be "engineered" in much the same way that a bridge is built or a pump is designed. Although the initial optimism has been reduced by the daunting challenges of building prosthetic devices, steady progress has been made. Here is a partial list of the replacement parts that either are now in use or near commercialization:

- bones and joints
- cartilage
- skin
- heart
- eye corneas
- lungs
- kidneys
- teeth
- blood vessels and blood
- heart valves
- hair
- ears (hearing aids)
- muscle controls (nerves)

A quiet revolution has occurred in the past fifteen years or so, as medical doctors and engineers collaborated on this growing list of prosthetics. Even more advances have been made in the area of analytical or diagnostic instruments. One example is computerized axial tomography (CAT) scanning, which can probe the human body to obtain visual diagrams of internal organs. Much of this type of work depends on top-notch electrical engineering.

Starting around 1980, genetic engineering arrived on the scene, creating a boom in pharmaceutical research that now goes under the general title of biotechnology. Engineers are rarely involved in actual genetic work. However, there are many applications involving advanced genetic manipulations in combination with manufacturing or research. These include:

- commercial-scale production of pharmaceutical agents
- industrial chemical production via microbes
- agricultural production with genetically altered plants
- production of sensors and diagnostic devices
- purification of biological compounds

There are a number of academic departments across the country where engineers can study these subjects. Some of them are available on an undergraduate basis; many of them are options or master's-level programs associated with chemical engineering departments. According to the Engineering Workforce Commission, 1,172 engineers received a B.S. in biomedical/bioengineering in 2000; there were also 528 M.S.E. graduates. Most of these engineers head toward the medical devices or pharmaceutical industry for jobs; many also go on to obtain a Ph.D.

Agricultural Engineering

Agricultural engineering applies the lessons of the factory to the farm. The mechanization of agricultural work has been a constant process for more than a century in the United States; agricultural production continues to go up, but the number of actual farmers continues to decline.

The roots of agricultural engineering as a distinct profession go back to the beginning of the twentieth century when a group of mostly mechanical engineers organized the American Society of Agricultural Engineers (ASAE). That organization now has about nine thousand members.

Like the founders of the profession, most agricultural engineers today are involved in developing machines and vehicles for farming. Soil conservation, forestry, and food production are also key areas. ASAE defines nine technical divisions among its members:

1. *Aquacultural engineering*—the study of increased production of sea life such as fish farms and hatcheries.
2. *Bioengineering*—the application of biological science to plant and animal production.
3. *Electrical and electronic systems*—ranges from electronic control of processing systems to instruments for measuring irrigation, feeding, and harvesting.
4. *Food and process engineering*—the application of engineering principles to the processing, handling, packaging, and storage of foodstuffs.
5. *Forest engineering*—the enhancement of tree production and harvesting.
6. *Knowledge systems*—the use of advanced computer programs such as artificial intelligence to aid in production and processing.
7. *Power and machinery*—the traditional element of agricultural engineering focused on vehicle design and power supplies.
8. *Soil and water*—includes irrigation, drainage, fertilization, and water-resource management for agriculture.
9. *Structures and environment*—ranges from barn construction to the development of advanced feedlots for livestock or storage systems for crops.

As these examples show, agricultural engineering cuts across a broad range of engineering topics. The overall field has had moderately good job prospects for the past several years, notwith-standing the continuing grim news among farm owners. The number of homesteads and family farms has dropped precipitously over the past ten years and is predicted to continue to fall during the next decade. However, the amount of land for production—and jobs for engineers—has held fairly steady.

There were 624 B.S.E. degrees awarded in agricultural engineering in 2000; that is down slightly from the mid-1990s. An additional 147 students earned M.S.E. degrees in 2000.

Nuclear Engineering

Many commentators have spoken in recent years of the "extinction" of the nuclear industry in the United States following the accident at the Three Mile Island nuclear power plant in 1979. That accident caused the cancellation of dozens of construction projects; no new nuclear power plant has been ordered for construction in the United States since.

But the picture is much more complex than the ups and downs of the nuclear business among utility companies. First, the United States has a considerable involvement in plant construction abroad. Second, the U.S. Department of Defense continues to order new, smaller plants for use in nuclear-powered submarines and ships. Third, nuclear engineering also entails the design and construction of medical equipment for diagnosis and treatment of disease and for analytical instruments used in industry. Fourth, there are just over one hundred nuclear power plants in the country; the operation, maintenance, and repair of them occupies the efforts of thousands of workers. Fifth, the Defense Department has sponsored an elaborate system of production facilities to purify radioactive materials for the production of nuclear weapons (including the concentrated fuel pellets that are the source of power for commercial nuclear plants). This system, parts of which can be traced back to the days of the Manhattan Project during World War II, is in desperate need of repair and refurbishing. The U.S. Department of Energy, which runs the system at the behest of the Defense Department, estimates that this renovation will cost more than $100 billion over the next decade or so. That's going to be a lot of work for nuclear and other engineers.

The foregoing represents fairly definite tasks that require nuclear engineering talents. There are also some possibilities for future growth. One possibility is that new nuclear plants will be ordered. Few people have been counting on this in recent years, but the emergence of global warming as a world-threatening pollution problem has changed some opinions. Nuclear plants, of course, don't burn fuel and therefore don't produce carbon dioxide. Also, the commercial utility network in the United States is rapidly running out of capacity, and a new round of plant construction is currently under way. These new plants don't have to be nuclear-based, but some of them could be.

Job Opportunities

Notwithstanding the strong career potential, fewer and fewer students are studying nuclear engineering. B.S. graduating class sizes peaked at around five hundred in the late 1970s, and have been slipping ever since. If nuclear power comes back into favor, there will be almost immediate demand for new engineers. The latest effort by the engineering design companies that build power plants are a variety of "inherently safe" designs that run at lower pressures or use design innovations developed in recent years to improve the safety of the plants.

Nuclear engineering is dominated by the power industry, but that isn't the exclusive employment opportunity. Nuclear medicine is a broad field, involving therapy for diseases and analytical techniques for detecting illness. Instruments using nuclear energy in some form are widely used in laboratories and in industry for maintenance or analysis of materials. These applications, though employing relatively few engineers, represent a broad range of opportunity.

Nuclear engineering students study the engineering basics, then additional courses in physics, power plant design, materials, and electronics. The 130 B.S.E. graduates in 1994 were complemented by another 130 M.S.E. graduates. These graduates will find jobs with the electric utilities, the military (as civilian engineers or as commissioned officers), engineering/construction firms, environmental firms, and instrumentation manufacturers.

Marine/Ocean Engineering and Naval Architecture

How much of American industry is on, in, or near the sea? Ships, of course, including the hundreds of craft that the United States Navy operates, are a major element. But there are also the offshore oil-drilling business, aquaculture, port design, undersea pipelines and telecommunications, dams, locks, and canals. Moreover, it is widely expected that the use of the world's oceans and waterways will increase in the future, if only because the technology to live or work in the ocean has only recently become available.

One example of this is the mining of naturally concentrated metallic nodules deep in ocean rifts. About a decade ago experimental submersible vessels discovered that there were volcanic vents that reached deep into the earth's core at the bottom of the Pacific Ocean. One day the mining of these nodules may be an important source of metals.

Another not-so-farfetched application concerns a technology known as OTEC, which stands for ocean thermal energy conversion. Researchers have known for decades that the difference in temperature between the water at the ocean's surface and the water several hundred feet below could be used to drive energy-generating turbines. (It can be used simultaneously to produce salt-free water.) OTEC was experimented with during the days of high-priced energy in the 1970s. It was found to be possible but too expensive at that time. If energy prices rise in the future, OTEC may once again look attractive.

It is ironic to speak of such futuristic technologies while discussing naval architecture, since this profession is centuries old. People have built ships since before the beginning of recorded history. Today, in the United States, ship design and construction is relatively quiet, except for the military. The United States Navy has some five hundred vessels, but there is talk today of decommissioning many of them and replacing only a few. The market for recreational ships, such as motorboats and sailing yachts, is also relatively small, but steadier in employment prospects.

These three engineering disciplines—marine and ocean engineering and naval architecture—have subtle differences in their outlook:

• *Marine engineering* is generally concerned with mechanical systems on board ships, such as the propulsion system, controls, and heating and cooling. Some of this technology also applies to stationary equipment at or in the ocean.

- *Naval architecture* is more concerned with the design and construction of hulls. Knowledge of the fluid dynamics of a vessel coursing through water is essential. Obviously there is a strong overlap between marine engineering and naval architecture. The distinctions between them are similar to those between mechanical engineers who design jet turbines and aerospace engineers who design aircraft powered by the turbines.

- *Ocean engineering* has been likened to civil engineering with wet feet. Ocean engineers are concerned with structures—such as ports, drilling platforms, or pipelines—next to or in oceans. Basic construction technology must be studied, along with the special effects of tides, saltwater, and sea life on ocean structures.

Job Opportunities and Education

Shipbuilding and ocean exploration are international businesses, with firms on many different continents and opportunities to travel the world. These businesses are also highly competitive, and the United States maritime industry has not fared well outside of military contracting. Most shipbuilding for freight transportation, for example, is carried out in the Far East. Nevertheless, as the volume of shipping increases due to greater international trade, the industry could revive in coming years.

The training for marine engineering and naval architecture covers engineering fundamentals, as well as fluid dynamics, energy and propulsion systems, and control. Marine engineers have an edge over naval architects in the job market because maritime engineers receive training in propulsion that can be transferred to utility plants or other land-based power systems. Ocean engineering is often closely associated with civil engineering programs, and the studies are similar, involving materials and structures and construction technology.

Most schools for marine/ocean engineering and naval architecture, naturally enough, are in states on the nation's shores—the West and East Coasts and the Gulf of Mexico. The United States Navy provides employment opportunities and training for its engineering officers. It also hires a large number of engineers for civilian employment at its major ports, including Newport News, Virginia, and San Diego, California.

Safety and Fire Protection Engineering

Risk and technology often go hand in hand. Many problems that engineering addresses involve dangers that must be considered before a design is completed or a building is built. A good example can be found in the chemical industry, where chemical businesses routinely work with hazardous intermediate chemicals in order to produce a final product that might be as safe as water.

Good engineering and safe engineering are the same thing. Nevertheless, many engineered processes or products are improved by having a safety specialist involved in the planning. Many safety engineers work for, or are closely associated with, the insurance business. Before providing an insurance policy, an insurance firm will often have safety specialists review a business's factories or products, making recommendations to the client to improve the safety of the process or product. In the short term, this analysis can result in lower insurance premiums; in the long term, it can result in fewer accidents, a safer workplace, and a more profitable business.

There are relatively few engineering departments in the country that offer specific courses in safety engineering. Usually they are part of industrial engineering or engineering management programs. There are also a variety of programs in safety from such nonengineering departments as industrial relations. After graduation there are numerous programs sponsored by insurance companies, research foundations, and professional organizations such as the American Society of Safety Engineers (ASSE). Safety engineering courses focus on such areas as accident prevention, the design of safe manufacturing equipment, and industrial codes and standards.

Interest in safety engineering has increased greatly over the past fifteen years or so. The United States Occupational Safety and Health Administration (OSHA) put federal enforcement behind national workplace safety rules. (OSHA is also a good place to gain work experience.) More recently the explosive growth in insurance costs and insurance awards has made safety a conscious issue with many industrial managers. ASSE has grown steadily in recent years, reaching thirty thousand members currently.

Safety engineering work requires a close understanding of the general rules of safe function or operation and familiarity with thousands of rules and technical standards for proper procedures. Research into such topics as inherently safe processes and human-machine interfaces further boosts the professionalism of the field.

A field closely related to safety engineering is fire protection engineering. These engineers, following study in any of a number of B.S. engineering programs, can also study fire protection engineering at several schools that offer master's degree programs. Employment opportunities range from chemical and petrochemical plants, to insurance companies, to suppliers of fire safety equipment for buildings, homes, and factories.

Optical Engineering

Lasers. Fiber optics. Space telescopes. Microwave communications. Microelectronics fabrication. The list of applications of optics in the modern world is long and growing. As yet, there are only a few B.S. programs and a few more M.S. or Ph.D. programs at schools for optical engineering. But there are quite a few engineers and scientists who specialize in the field. There are about seven thousand members in the International Society for Optical Engineering and about ten thousand in the Optical Society of America.

Optical engineering involves understanding and working with the properties of light. New materials, such as ruby lasers and polymeric optical fibers, make it possible to generate new forms of light and to carry that light along wires.

The optical industry is closely allied with electronics and electrical engineering, since so many of the applications are in microelectronics and instrumentation. Students who want to pursue a career in optical engineering are advised to take extra courses in mathematics and physics in high school and during their undergraduate years. The best job opportunities develop after obtaining a master's or higher degree.

Much optical work is done by scientists, primarily physicists, who investigate new ways to produce or use light. Optical engineers then transform this research into commercial products. The job outlook is excellent, since many of the latest advances in microelectronics depend on optical principles.

Other Engineering Specialties

The fields of study mentioned above still do not complete the list of engineering professions. The following specialties tend to be very small or have only limited presence on college campuses. In the latter case, students usually major in one of the larger engineering disciplines in college and then specialize through professional affiliation with an engineering society. Often the engineering society will offer technical seminars or continuing education courses that provide the necessary training for the specialty. There are many specialties that meet these criteria.

Automotive Engineering

This field is not taught at any accredited college, yet the Society of Automotive Engineers has nearly fifty thousand members—a very large group in engineering circles. The existence of this professional organization is a testament to the size and importance of the automotive and transportation industries in the United States. The automobile dominates the field in terms of professional interest. These engineers are concerned with engines, structural components, fuels, lubricants, suspensions, and related topics. Because these elements are common to other vehicles, automotive engineers also work in the aerospace industry or for manufacturers of heavy-construction equipment, farm vehicles, mass-transit systems, and trucks.

Textile Engineering

With several programs, mostly in schools in the South, textile engineers are trained to manage the design and operation of the weaving and cutting equipment that textile manufacturers use. Textiles, as a material, involve much more than clothing. One can also find textile engineers at high-tech aerospace firms, where they are concerned with handling the glass or carbon fibers that are used with plastic resins to make composite materials such as fiberglass.

Energy Engineering

The energy industry is huge, encompassing oil producers, utilities, power systems, solar energy production, batteries for electric storage, and many other forms of energy. Mechanical, electrical, and industrial engineers are well represented. Most energy engineers, on the other hand, are concerned with the use and conservation of energy. They might help develop plans to insulate a building, the better to conserve the energy needed to heat and cool it; or they might assist in a factory's plan to build its own power station, rather than buying power from a utility. The Association of Energy Engineers, with about six thousand members, is the leading professional organization.

Heating, Ventilating, Air-Conditioning, and Refrigeration Engineering

This long name, usually abbreviated as HVACR, refers to the climate control systems of homes, buildings, and large vehicles. HVACR engineers, like energy engineers, are concerned with the use and conservation of energy. HVACR engineers also help create the conditions that make people comfortable and safe—an environment with the right temperature, humidity, cleanliness, and lighting. These concerns usually fall under the technical term psychometrics. Most HVACR engineers work for construction companies, building management firms, or equipment suppliers. The American Society of Heating, Refrigeration, and

Air-Conditioning Engineers, Inc., has nearly sixty thousand members.

Systems Engineering/Operations Research

These two programs exist at many colleges, but there are relatively few professionals who identify themselves as systems engineers or operations researchers. Both programs tend to be more emphasized at M.S. or Ph.D. levels.

The field came about as scientists and engineers realized over the past century that a different skill is needed when a large, complex organization or structure is involved. An airline is a good example. There are mechanical engineers for the aircraft themselves and transportation engineers for airports, but who pulls together all the necessary elements—people, planes, baggage, fuel and spare parts, food and services? Someone must handle the large volume of customers and get the maximum profit. This is one example of the problems that systems engineering and operations research address.

Other topics include space or satellite programs, the design of new factories or production lines, or military equipment programs. The skills employed include computer programming and mathematical theory, combined with experimentation and observation. There are about twelve thousand members of the Institute for Operations Research and Management Sciences.

Engineering History/Technical Writing

The history of science and technology is intricate and fascinating, and it has only recently become popular on college campuses. Most teachers of the history of technology have undergraduate degrees in history or another of the liberal arts, but the advantages of having engineering training are obvious. Aside from academic positions at colleges and universities, historians of technology are employed by major corporations to write company histories and by journals and periodicals. The Society for the History of Technology has about three thousand members.

Technical writing is similar to engineering history in that the main activity is writing, and also in that most professionals do not have an engineering degree (however, it is a benefit to have one). Technical writing covers a broad range of topics, including journalism, advertising copywriting, documentation for user's manuals, and contract preparation. A large segment of the technical writing field today is devoted to providing the documentation that goes along with computer programs. Most programs are not self-explanatory; they require a manual that guides the customer through the program steps. The Society for Technical Communications, Inc., has about ten thousand members.

6

ENGINEERING TECHNOLOGY

ENGINEERING TECHNOLOGY (E.T.), sometimes called industrial technology, is becoming much more highly prominent today. As increased technology is employed in more parts of the American economy, more people with technical training are needed.

Most of the major engineering disciplines—mechanical, electrical, computer, civil, chemical, aerospace, and manufacturing—have a counterpart degree in technology. There are programs and jobs for mechanical engineering technologists, electrical engineering technologists, and so forth. Most of the details of the various engineering disciplines in the preceding chapters also hold for engineering technologists. Therefore, only the general situation for E.T. will be reviewed, with some examples of specific types.

The Pros and Cons of Engineering Technology

The formal definition of engineering technology, as espoused by the American Society for Engineering Education, is as follows:

Engineering technology is that part of the technological field which requires the application of scientific and engineering knowledge and methods combined with technical skills in support of engineering activities; it lies in the area between the craftsman and the engineer in the part closest to the engineer.

Engineering technology makes sense for some people:

- Those who don't have the time or money to attend college full-time for four years.
- Those who enjoy science, math, and technology but don't feel confident enough of their aptitude in these subjects to study engineering.
- Those who want to work on the maintenance or operation of technical equipment, but are sure that they don't want to work on the design of such equipment or on research for new types of equipment.

In general, E.T. degrees are available at associate (two-year) and bachelor (four-year) levels. Many people define two-year graduates as technicians and four-year graduates as technologists. In reality the job titles may be intermingled. In fact the technologist may wind up being called an engineer.

There are a few programs that offer master's degrees, but only a very small number of students obtain them. Many two-year E.T. programs are offered at community or junior colleges. Many programs are also offered with full or partial sponsorship of local employers who can provide co-op programs that combine work with study.

In general the curriculum for engineering technology has basic math and science courses and then a number of courses tailored to specific industrial applications such as electrical systems, electronic components, machine tools, instrumentation, construction, or manufacturing methods. With this training, graduates can move directly into jobs as technicians, production personnel, or service specialists in a wide range of industries. Many employers like the idea of having an employee who is ready to work once hired; often, graduates of four-year engineering programs need a certain amount of on-the-job training before they begin to be productive.

Lacking the more comprehensive courses in higher math and science, most E.T. graduates are not equipped to work as design or development engineers. With experience and additional training, it is possible for technologists to get design work, if they so desire. And, the option of taking additional schooling to get the full engineering degree is always available. No doors are slammed shut because of prior experience as a technologist. However, certain engineering specialties will grant licensing or certification only if the candidate has graduated with a minimum of a four-year degree from an accredited engineering program.

In one area, technologists and engineers are often competing for the same job: manufacturing supervision. Many E.T. graduates work as manufacturing specialists, just as do graduates of programs in industrial or mechanical engineering. The Society of Manufacturing Engineers, many of whose members have E.T. degrees, has nearly eighty thousand members.

If you think that you could handle the requirements of an engineering program or an E.T. program equally well, and you are willing to spend four years in school, it is probably best to pursue the engineering degree. An engineering degree provides more options and can put you on a faster track for management positions. Most employers reviewing comparable students, one with an E.T. degree and one with an engineering degree, will take the engineer first.

Pay is usually less, by about $2,000 to $3,000 annually for starting E.T. grads with four-year degrees than for B.S. engineers. That difference is sometimes made up over time as the E.T. graduates gain experience with their employers.

Types of Engineering Technology Degrees

The range of engineering technology degrees is, in some ways, even broader than that of engineers. Some of the degrees overlap; for instance, to work in the automotive industry one can obtain a mechanical engineering technology degree and also an automotive technology degree. The Accreditation Board for Engineering and Technology (ABET) accredits most E.T. programs, but often they are created more rapidly than the accreditation program can adjust. Therefore, some programs are graduating students before the full accreditation is garnered. A list of E.T. degrees follows. If you are limited to a certain area or number of schools, it is wise to check with those schools to see if other E.T. degrees are offered.

Engineering Technology Degree Titles
aeronautical, astronautical
air-conditioning, heating, and refrigeration
architectural
automotive
chemical
civil, highway, surveying
computer
construction
drafting, design
electrical
electromechanical

electronic
engineering science
environmental
general
industrial and manufacturing
marine
materials
mechanical
mining, metallurgical
nuclear
welding

As you can see, the list is a long one, and new degrees are continually being added. There is no definitive count of how many E.T. graduates there are, but the Engineering Workforce Commission, which provides the most comprehensive accounting, recorded 8,415 four-year graduates in 2,000 and 11,354 two-year graduates. Thus, for every E.T. graduate, there are about five engineering graduates, including those with master's and Ph.D. degrees.

Work Environments

Although engineers work predominantly in manufacturing or construction, they also find opportunities in consulting, business services, and government. Most E.T. graduates work in manufacturing and construction exclusively. With the practical training they receive, E.T. graduates are well equipped to perform many functions.

- *Production and maintenance.* E.T. graduates can move off the campus and onto the factory floor or construction site as supervisors, maintenance specialists, instrumentation technicians, and quality-control managers. American manufacturers are straining mightily to upgrade the quality and cost-effectiveness of their production lines, and more engineering technologists are being hired in this effort.

• *Construction management.* Construction technologists could have either general experience in handling construction jobs, or specialize in a particular aspect, such as heating, ventilating, and air-conditioning (HVAC) systems, electrical systems, and the like.

• *Technical service.* When a manufacturer sells a particularly complex piece of equipment, such as a large computer or the instrumentation system for a factory line, many technicians and technologists go along to help with the installation. After the system is up and running, most sales contracts call for the supplier to provide regular maintenance. Sometimes the equipment is so complex and the maintenance needs so steady, that the supplier stations the maintenance technologist at the installation site permanently. However, technical service can also require lots of travel. For some specialists it offers a way of working part-time at a substantial salary because they are on call and work only when needed.

• *Quality analysis and laboratory services.* Most production lines require constant checking to make sure that products are being put together correctly. In addition, there are numerous independent laboratories that offer analytical services to check on the quality, consistency, and performance of products. These efforts require sophisticated instruments and good judgment, and E.T. graduates are often called on to perform the task.

These are the main areas of employment, but they aren't meant to be exclusive. Inspectors (for private companies or for government agencies), testing and quality-control specialists, and those working in the operation of complex machinery, record-keeping, surveying or mapping for construction companies, research assistance, and a wide variety of technical support positions are all very real possibilities. Getting other types of work, or going on into design or other areas traditionally thought to be the province of engineers, is up to the initiative of the engineering technologist.

Special mention deserves to be made with regard to computers and computer technology. The range of users of computing equipment is growing so rapidly that it is still possible to get a job as a computer specialist with little formal training in computer science. You can become a technologist by gaining experience on computers either through school or simply by working with computers wherever you can. Of course, the more training you get, the better your career prospects will be.

There is no question that the two-year associate degree is significantly less comprehensive than the four year degree, whether it is four years of E.T. or four years of engineering. But the advantage of the two-year degree is that you can get a job that pays fairly well ($20,000 per year or better) with the option of continuing your education to get a full four-year degree. It may also be possible to find an employer who will help fund the continuation of your education.

7

Engineering Education

When you make plans to attend college and study engineering, several key factors should influence your choices:

- the type of engineering program you will enter
- the quality of the school
- the prospects for employment or advanced schooling after graduation
- your personal preferences in living and learning

This chapter will help you begin investigating these issues. The next section will outline the types of engineering programs available and discuss the other points mentioned above. Keep in mind that the most important decision is to study engineering. The engineering program, the school you choose, and the other factors are of lesser importance. Once you get started on the road to an engineering career, you can change directions in terms of schooling, employment, or long-term career goals. The most important step is the first one—choosing an engineering education.

The Engineering Curriculum

Nearly all engineering programs begin with introductory courses in physics and chemistry and a math course geared to the student's incoming level of education. Usually the first math courses are two terms of calculus. Some students, already well trained in calculus, take the next level up, which could range from linear algebra to differential equations. Because the use of statistics in quality control is now so critical to manufacturing, many engineering students should take this course as well. Other students, not being well prepared in mathematics, may need a precalculus course, followed by the other math courses.

By spring, the college freshman has made a preliminary choice for an engineering program. In the sophomore year, the student begins taking courses in that engineering program. There is usually an introductory course that deals with the general principles of the engineering discipline. This class may be offered concurrently with other specific engineering courses. Another level of science courses is also taken, which might be more chemistry or physics or courses such as computer science, geology, or biology.

In the junior year, a large part of the curriculum is taken up with engineering courses. By now the math requirements are usually fulfilled. Often these courses have substantial laboratory requirements—three or six hours per week.

In the senior year, the final courses of the undergraduate program are taken. Usually these courses will have a heavy orientation toward design. Students might be assigned courses in which they design actual objects or systems: aircraft wings, chemical manu-facturing processes, building construction specifications.

Along the way most colleges specify a minimum set of electives in technical and nontechnical areas. Although engineering students are traditionally thought of as avoiding literature or art courses, these courses are heavily represented. Writing and communication skills are also emphasized, both in nontechnical electives and in engineering courses. For example, in their junior-year laboratory courses, students might be required to present the results of an experimental program orally before the class. Studying a foreign language is usually not a requirement, but many engineering students find it desirable to do so, especially if they plan on advanced schooling or a career that involves foreign travel.

Technical Electives

It is with the technical electives that students have the greatest opportunities to tailor their engineering education. Some schools have formal college major/college minor structures, in which a student majors in one topic while fulfilling a set of requirements for a minor. Some students find it desirable to carry a double major. By choosing elective courses carefully, one can fulfill the course requirements for two separate departments.

More often, though, it is through these technical electives that an engineering student directs his or her training to specific engineering specialties. Civil engineers, for example, can choose to specialize in building construction, environmental work, or materials design through the courses they choose. Mechanical engineers can specialize in aerospace or microelectronics. Electrical engineers can specialize in circuit design, power systems, or industrial process control.

Choosing a School

There are about thirty-five hundred colleges and universities across the country; about five hundred of these (including branch campuses) have one or several engineering or engineering technology programs. Which school should you choose?

The first step is to make decisions about your personal preferences. You may want to attend a school in the immediate vicinity of your home or a school that is far away. You may want a school in the country or one in an urban setting. Obviously the expense of the school is a major factor, and public universities are usually considerably less expensive than private schools. Once you make some of these decisions, you are then ready to consider the potential advantages of specific schools.

Types of Schools

Although all schools consider themselves unique in some way, there are four main types of engineering schools. These are (1) research universities, (2) engineering schools, (3) state universities, (4) private schools.

Research universities have large, comprehensive science and engineering departments. They also have graduate-level programs that attract funding from the federal government and private industry. The top researchers in the country teach at these schools, although they usually teach only graduate-level students, not undergraduates.

The engineering universities are those whose student body is dominated by the engineering program. Many of these schools include the words "institute of technology" in their name. There are a number of liberal arts departments, but the school's focus is on engineering. There are many advantages to attending a school with a large number of fellow engineers, but that is also its main drawback. Some students simply don't want to spend all their time at college with students in the same basic program.

The third type of school, the state university, is the source of most engineering graduates. Many of these schools are land-grant colleges founded as the American West began to open up in the late nineteenth century. They have tens of thousands of students of all types. The schools are usually affordable, especially for residents of that state, and the quality of education can be high. Some state universities are major research powerhouses in their own right.

The fourth category, private colleges and universities, has the widest range of capabilities and quality. Some are quite good; some have only a few types of engineering programs. Some are tailored to the employment needs of major corporations in the school's area.

Again, a certain amount of personal preference enters into the college-choice question. Would you prefer to attend a large school or a small one? Do you want a school where most of your peers are also engineering students or one where they are not? Would you enjoy a school where laboratories and facilities are not so large but where teachers pay great personal attention to their students?

Other Selection Criteria

All schools that offer accredited engineering degrees must meet the minimum requirements of the Accreditation Board of Engineering and Technology (ABET). Check that the accreditation is in order at the school you might attend. Beyond that, check the quality and availability of laboratories and computer equipment. Most schools across the country have had tremendous difficulty keeping up-to-date labs and computer systems because of the high cost of such equipment. But, by developing formal or informal alliances with corporate sponsors, many schools have been able to upgrade their laboratories and computer systems.

The status and reputation of the engineering professors themselves is a difficult issue to address. A very prestigious research university may have top engineers on the faculty, but their interactions with undergraduate students may be minimal or nonexistent. One thing to check closely is how many of the courses are actually taught by a full professor, versus the use of teaching assistants.

The rest of the school, outside of the engineering program, is also important, since many of your courses will be held there. Compare the size and types of liberal arts programs at different schools. Find out how well the engineering students are integrated into the overall student body. At some schools the engineering departments tend to be isolated from the rest of the school (which can have advantages and disadvantages of its own).

A final, but very important, element to check in undergraduate facilities is the quality of the placement office. Some schools have a room with a few books; this is less than minimally acceptable. Many have an office where recruiters from corporations or the public sector visit to interview seniors. These interviews may be supplemented with training and preparation for writing résumés and conducting interviews. Compare the number and quality of firms represented at the placement offices at each school. Check also how successful the school is in placing B.S.E. graduates in postgraduate programs.

Alternatives to the Four-Year Program

Most high school graduates going to college plan to attend for four years, take summers off, and graduate. However, there are a variety of alternatives. One of the more important of these for engineering students is the co-op program. Co-op (short for "cooperative") is a method of paying for school while you are attending and getting training that might be directly related to your ultimate career. Co-ops are usually arranged so that the student graduates with a B.S.E. degree in five years rather than four. Usually each term is alternated with a term of working with local employers (including summers). The work can range from technician's tasks to being a "junior engineer" who assists working engineers in their tasks.

Co-ops are valuable for engineering students because they can provide training similar to the work that full-fledged engineers perform. Many schools have provisions for co-op education; there are also several where the co-op program is stressed.

Another type of program that some students use is a "3-2" program leading to a master's degree. This often exists at schools that, individually, do not have a fully accredited engineering curriculum. The school accepts students who take all the preparatory courses for an engineering degree during the first three years (i.e., all the math, science, and liberal arts electives). The student then attends another school where the necessary engineering courses are taken.

The P.E. License

A professional engineer's (P.E.) license has the same function as an M.D. title for medical doctors or L.L.D. or J.D. for lawyers. To be a professional engineer, one must pass an examination on engineering fundamentals, usually taken at the end of one's undergraduate program or immediately after. After passing this exam the student becomes an "engineer in training" (E.I.T.). Then, after being employed as an engineer for several years (usually a minimum of three), the E.I.T. takes a second exam that tests general knowledge of engineering practices. Some schools make provisions in the senior-year curriculum for the E.I.T. exam.

Professional licensing has some practical value and much symbolic value. For certain types of engineers, such as construction specialists who handle public-works projects, a license is necessary. Someone at the firm doing the work must be licensed. His or her professional seal on the final blueprints signifies that a fully qualified professional engineer has examined the plans and approved them. Obviously if you are going to work on your own in public-works construction, you need your P.E. license. If you join a larger firm, with P.E.s already on staff, you may not need the license, but the firm may want you to get one as soon as you can.

The P.E. license also has symbolic value. Engineers who have one show that they are serious about their work and consider themselves true professionals. There are a few situations when having the P.E. license results in slightly higher pay, but this is the exception rather than the rule.

Some people view engineers with a P.E. license as the only true engineers. The importance of the license is a matter of opinion. However, most corporations do not require their engineers to be licensed. Thus only about 15 percent of working engineers have one. P.E. licensing is administered by state organizations that are banded together as the National Council of Engineering Examiners. There is also another organization, the National Society of Professional Engineers, all of whose members are licensed.

Financial Aid

Financing should not be an impossible obstacle to obtaining an engineering degree. Although the costs of a college education are high and growing higher every year, scholarships, grants, work-study programs, and other forms of financial aid are available. The better your academic record, the more opportunities appear. Women and minority students have many sources of funding for engineering education in addition to the ones available to all students.

Engineering usually has a special status in the view of the federal government because of its importance to the manufacturing capability of the country and the need for supplying high-tech military equipment. At this time there are no special financial programs from the federal government for engineering students at the undergraduate level. At the master's and higher levels, however, there is funding from the National Science Foundation and other sources to help engineers continue their education.

Private industry helps out by sponsoring a variety of scholarships for engineers. A special variation of the work-study program is the availability of summer work for college juniors and, sometimes, sophomores. Many companies use these programs as a means of introducing the company to potential recruits. The availability of these temporary jobs depends on the state of the economy and the demand for engineering graduates. When the number of engineering students falls, companies try to increase the summer openings to attract more students to the various engineering disciplines.

Check in reference books, with high school advisers, and with the financial-aid counselors at the college you would like to attend for information on scholarships, work-study, and summer jobs. Don't give up until you have obtained the financing you need to attend school.

What to Do Now

Assuming that you are a sophomore or junior in high school, there are several things you can do now to prepare for studying engineering.

An obvious first step is to take as many science and math courses as you can. You can't overprepare in this sense because all the math and science you learn will be applied in an engineering program. You should do well in these courses, although there may be many valid reasons for getting less than "A"s all along the way. If you don't do well, ask yourself if you gave the courses your best effort, or if there were other reasons you did not excel. Be confident of your abilities in math and science.

There is an educational association sponsored by the professional engineering societies that offers a big boost to high school students considering studying engineering. This association is JETS—the Junior Engineering Technical Society. JETS sponsors academic competitions, design contests, workshops, and other activities that help high school students learn about engineering. One such program, the Tests of Engineering Aptitude, Mathematics, and Science (TEAMS) competition, encourages higher order thinking, leadership skills, academic excellence, and working successfully as a team to solve problems faced by engineers and scientists. JETS also sponsors the National Engineering Aptitude Search, a guidance test that helps students gauge how well prepared they are for studying engineering. Its guidance program offers activities and materials that can be used in math, science, and technology clubs at high schools.

JETS also helps organize contact between working engineers and high school students contemplating an engineering career. Contacting a working engineer can be a valuable help in determining what kind of engineering work you might want to do. Ask family and friends for a reference to engineers. Then call or write to them, asking for an interview and perhaps a tour of their company's facilities. Or, call or write directly to manufacturing or construction companies in your area, seeking the same things. Getting this exposure will help you find out where your interests are and will provide a role model for carrying you through your engineering program. Good luck!

APPENDIX A

Recommended Reading

Adams, James L. *Flying Buttresses, Entropy and O-Rings: The World of an Engineer.* Cambridge, MA: Harvard University Press, 1991.

American Association of Engineering Societies. The *International Directory of Engineering Societies and Related Organizations.* Washington, DC, 2000.

Basta, Nicholas. *Environmental Jobs for Engineers and Scientists.* New York: Wiley, 1992.

Campbell-Kelly, Martin, and William Aspray. *Computer: A History of the Information Machine* (Sloan Technology Series). New York: Basic Books, 1996.

CEIP Fund. *Complete Guide to Environmental Careers in the 21st Century.* Washington, DC: Island Press, 1998.

Florman, Samuel C. *Blaming Technology.* New York: St. Martin's Press, 1981.

———. *The Civilized Engineer.* New York: St. Martin's Press, 1987.

————. *The Existential Pleasures of Engineering.* New York: St. Martin's Press, 1976.

McMahon, A. Michal. *The Making of a Profession: A Century of Electrical Engineering in America.* New York: IEEE Press, 1984.

Manes, Stephen, and Paul Andrews. *Gates: How Microsoft's Mogul Reinvented an Industry.* New York: Doubleday, 1993.

Petroski, Henry. *The Evolution of Useful Things.* New York: Alfred Knopf, 1992.

————. *Remaking the World: Adventures in Engineering.* New York: Alfred Knopf, 1998.

————. *To Engineer is Human: The Role of Failure in Successful Design.* New York: St. Martin's Press, 1985.

Reynolds, Terry S. *Seventy-Five Years of Progress: A History of the American Institute of Chemical Engineers 1908–1983.* New York: American Institute of Chemical Engineers, 1983.

Rhodes, Richard, ed. *Visions of Technology: A Century of Vital Debate About Machines, Systems and the Human World.* New York: Simon & Schuster, 1999.

Sinclair, Bruce. *A Centennial History of the American Society of Mechanical Engineers 1880–1980.* Toronto: Toronto University Press, 1980.

Stewart, Robert E. *Seven Decades That Changed America: A History of the American Society of Agricultural Engineers.* St. Joseph, MI: ASAE, 1979.

Appendix B

Engineering and Technology Associations

Following is a list of associations mentioned in this book, along with a number of related groups. This list by no means represents the total number of engineering-related associations, which runs into the hundreds. A good reference for further inquiry is the 2000 edition of the *International Directory of Engineering Societies and Related Organizations*, published by the American Association of Engineering Societies. See Appendix A for details.

Most of these associations can provide you with educational or career-planning literature. The Junior Engineering Technical Society, listed below, has brief pamphlets describing most engineering fields.

Alliance for Engineering in Medicine and Biology
1101 Connecticut Ave. NW
Washington, DC 20036

American Academy of Environmental Engineers
130 Holiday Court, Ste. 100
Annapolis, MD 21401
410-266-3311
aaee.net

The American Ceramic Society
P.O. Box 6136
Westerville, OH 43086-6136
614-890-4700
Fax: 614-899-6109
info@acers.org

American Institute of Aeronautics and Astronautics
1801 Alexander Bell Dr., Ste. 500
Reston, VA 20191-4344
703-264-7500
800-639-AIAA
aiaa.org

American Institute of Chemical Engineers
3 Park Ave.
New York, NY 10016-5991
aiche.org

American Institute for Medical and Biological Engineering
1901 Pennsylvania Ave. NW, Ste. 401
Washington, DC 20006
202-496-9660
Fax: 202-466-8489
aimbe.org

American Institute of Mining, Metallurgical and Petroleum Engineers
3 Park Ave., 17th Floor
New York, NY 10016-5998
212-419-7676
aimeny.org

American Institute of Physics
335 E. 45th St.
New York, NY 10017
aip.org

American Institute of Plant Engineers
3975 Erie Ave.
Cincinnati, OH 45208
ocec.org

American Nuclear Society
555 N. Kensington Ave.
LaGrange Park, IL 60525
708-352-6611
ans.org

American Society of Agricultural Engineers
2950 Niles Rd.
St. Joseph, MI 49085
616-429-0300
asae.org

American Society of Civil Engineers
1801 Alexander Bell Dr.
Reston, VA 20191
800-548-2723
asce.org

American Society of Heating, Refrigerating, and Air-Conditioning
  Engineers, Inc. (ASHRAE)
1791 Tullie Circle NE
Atlanta, GA 30329
ashrae.org

ASME International (American Society of
  Mechanical Engineers)
3 Park Ave.
New York, NY 10016-5990
800-843-2763
asme.org

ASM International (American Society for Metals)
9639 Kinsmen Rd.
Metals Park, OH 44073
asminternational.org

American Society of Naval Engineers
1452 Duke St.
Alexandria, VA 22314

American Society of Safety Engineers
1800 E. Oakton St.
Des Plaines, IL 60018
asse.org

Institute of Electrical and Electronics Engineers, Inc.—USA
1828 L St. NW, Ste. 1202
Washington, DC 20036-5104
202-785-0017
Fax: 202-785-0835
ieee.org

IEEE Computer Society
1730 Massachusetts Ave. NW
Washington, DC 20036-1992
202-371-0101
Fax: 202-728-9614
computer.org

Institute of Industrial Engineers
25 Technology Park
Norcross, GA 30092
iienet.org

Institute for Operations Research and the Management
  Sciences
INFORMS
901 Elkridge Landing Rd., Ste. 400
Linthicum, MD 21090
800-446-3676

The Instrumentation, Systems and Automation Society
Education Services
67 Alexander Dr.
P.O. Box 12277
Research Triangle Park, NC 27709
isa.org

The International Society for Optical Engineering (SPIE)
P.O. Box 10
Bellingham, WA 98227-0010
360-676-3290
Fax: 360-647-1445
spie.org

Junior Engineering Technical Society (JETS)
1420 King St., Ste. 405
Alexandria, VA 22314-2715
jets.org

The Mining and Metallurgical Society of America
476 Wilson Ave.
Novato, CA 94947
415-897-1380
mmsa.net

The Minerals, Metals, and Materials Society (TMS)
184 Thorn Hill Rd.
Warrendale, PA 15086-7514
724-776-9000
Fax: 724-776-3770
tms.org

National Action Council for Minorities in Engineering, Inc.
    (NACME)
Empire State Building, 350 Fifth Ave., Ste. 2212
New York, NY 10118-2299
212-279-2626
nacme.org

National Institute of Ceramic Engineers
65 Ceramic Dr.
Columbus, OH 43214

National Society of Professional Engineers (NSPE)
1420 King St.
Alexandria, VA 22314
nspe.org

Optical Society of America
2010 Massachusetts Ave. NW
Washington, DC 20036
202-223-8130
osa.org

SAE International (Society of Automotive Engineers)
Headquarters
400 Commonwealth Dr.
Warrendale, PA 15096-0001
sae.org

Society of Fire Protection Engineers
7315 Wisconsin Ave., Ste. 1225 W
Bethesda, MD 20814
301-718-2910
Fax: 301-718-2242
sfpe.org

Society of Manufacturing Engineers
One SME Dr.
Dearborn, MI 48121
sme.org

Society of Naval Architects and Marine Engineers
601 Pavonia Ave.
Jersey City, NJ 07306
201-798-4800
800-798-2188
Fax: 201-798-4975

Society of Plastics Engineers
14 Fairchild Dr.
Brookfield, CT 06804
4spe.org

Society of Women Engineers
230 E. Ohio St., Ste. 400
Chicago, IL 60611-3265
312-596-5223
Fax: 312-644-8557
swe.org

About the Author

For the past twenty-five years, Nicholas Basta has worked as a business and technology journalist in New York, focusing on manufacturing, government policies, environmental activities, computer technology, and professional careers. Most recently he was vice president, editorial, for VerticalNet, Inc., an Internet-based business services company. He has written hundreds of articles appearing in engineering and business publications. His books include *The Environmental Career Guide: Job Opportunities with the Earth in Mind* (John Wiley, 1991) and *Major Options: The Student's Guide to Linking College Majors and Career Opportunities* (HarperCollins, 1991).

Basta graduated in 1977 from Princeton University with a B.S. degree in chemical engineering.